SUMO

What people say about Paul McGee's SUMO presentations and workshops ...

'May I on behalf of everyone at Manchester United who attended your session, thank you for a great presentation. The feedback has been excellent and all very positive, and I know the ideas within your SUMO message are greatly appreciated.'
Kenneth Merrett
Club Secretary, Manchester United FC

'You inspired the audience with your SUMO techniques. You were practical, motivational and entertaining.'
Miles Standish
Managing Director, UK Life and Pensions, Towry Law Group

'The feedback has been unbelievable! Delegates were using some of the seven questions during the conference. Lots of fun, but at the same time, lots of learning.'
Philip Turner
Operations Director, NHS

'Paul, you did not disappoint. Staff morale needed to be lifted during this period of change and your approach injected new life into our conference. Aside from your truly motivational presentation, we also appreciated the copious amounts of humour.'
Fiona Tuffs
Marketing and Development Director,
North East Chamber of Commerce

'I know that many people personally thanked you on the night for your inspired message and how they had been challenged to change the way they deal with situations. However, it is remarkable that two months on, the messages that you gave us are still remembered and talked about. Our teaching staff have gone on to give positive "can do" messages to the pupils and frequently refer to SUMO and how we can "Move On" to greater things both as individuals and as a school.'
Julia Carey
Headteacher, Victoria Community Technology School

'SUMO may sound very simple but it is the truth of life!'
Archana Schafer
Managing Partner, EMA International, Dubai

'After listening to your presentation I have made some radical changes to my coaching plans and techniques. You have opened up my way of thinking with your extremely motivational and thought-provoking SUMO approach.'
Mark Tolley
Sports Coach, Cumbria County Council

'Your day in the store made a big difference. The average score of how people felt able to cope with change moved from 71% to 94%; a great move, especially starting from a reasonable base. Your SUMO ideas are frequently used.'
Paul Sanders
Store Manager, Marks & Spencer

'Paul McGee speaks from the heart and has a passion that makes his content even more powerful. This passion isn't one of those "showman types" but is based on a deep-seated belief in what he has to say and what he has to offer his audience.'
Paul Bridle
President of the International Federation for Professional Speakers

'Out of all the presentations at the conference, your SUMO principles had the most impact on me. SUMO is spreading like wildfire in South Africa as I tell all and sundry! Thanks for sharing your wisdom with us.'

Melodie de Jager
Director, The BG Connexion Ltd, South Africa

'Paul, you're not a motivational or inspirational speaker ... I actually think you're a life-changing speaker. You give people the tools to change their lives.'

Nigel Risner
Television presenter and speaker

'We live in a complex world. Paul McGee's messages stand out because they're clear, simple and above all they work. We have a short time on this planet and we need to make the most of it. SUMO shows you how. By applying these ideas I believe you can make a BIG difference in every area of your life, personally and professionally.'

Marie Mosely
Business Psychologist

'How can we sum up this book and the SUMO approach to life? Quite simply. No bull. No boredom. Just brilliant ideas. Get ready to SUMO and enjoy the ride.'
Steve McDermott and Philip Hesketh
Co-creators of The Confident Club

Paul's SUMO principles are essential life tools, nothing less. I refer to his seven questions on an almost daily basis. They have been massively useful for dealing with issues both personally and professionally. Paul, I cannot thank you enough.'
David Thomas
International speaker, author and memory world record holder

SUMO

(Shut Up, Move On)

The straight talking guide to creating and enjoying a brilliant life

By Paul McGee

Illustrations by Fiona Griffiths

Reprinted October 2006, January 2007, August 2007

First published 2006 by
Capstone Publishing Limited (a Wiley Company)
The Atrium
Southern Gate
Chichester
West Sussex
PO19 8SQ
www.wileyeurope.com
Email (for orders and customer service enquires): cs-books@wiley.co.uk

CIP catalogue records for this book are available from the British Library and
the US Library of Congress

ISBN 13: 978-1-84112-711-8 (PB)

Typeset in 11/15 pt Meridien by Sparks, Oxford – www.sparks.co.uk

Printed and bound in Great Britain by TJ International Ltd, Padstow, Cornwall
This book is printed on acid-free paper responsibly manufactured from
sustainable forestry in which at least two trees are planted for each one used
for paper production.

Dedication

To Paul 'The Philosopher'
with deep gratitude and appreciation
for sharing your friendship, wisdom and laughter.
From The Sumo Guy

Proverbs 18 v 24

The SUMO Principles

Seven questions to help you SUMO

1. Where is this issue on a scale of 1–10?

2. How important will this be in six months time?

3. Is my response appropriate and effective?

4. How can I influence or improve the situation?

5. What can I learn from this?

6. What will I do differently next time?

7. What can I find that's positive in this situation?

By applying the SUMO principles to your life, you will discover how to:

- Define what success means for you

- Be successful AND maintain a balanced life

- Respond honestly and appropriately to set-backs and challenges

- Maintain your motivation after your initial enthusiasm has worn off

- Develop successful relationships with others

- Overcome thinking patterns that can sabotage your success

SHUT UP, Move On – and enjoy the journey.

Contents

About the Author

PAUL McGEE is an international speaker, workshop leader, author of books and audio programmes, and proud creator of SUMO (Shut Up, Move On®).

Paul's main aim in life is to help others SUMO, whilst having plenty of fun in the process. He has spread the word about SUMO in 20 countries across the globe. Paul has also worked with major organizations in both public and private sectors world wide. Paul is founder member and fellow of the Professional Speakers Association, a fellow of the Institute of Sales and Marketing and an associate of the Chartered Institute of Personal Development.

Preface

When a baby is born there are numerous questions that are immediately asked. Is the baby healthy? How much does it weigh? Have they decided on a name? I'm going to let you into a secret. Authors can be a little bit like parents of a newborn child. Once their book is published, a flood of questions well up instantly. Are the major stores stocking it? Will people find it a good read? Most importantly of all, will it sell?

Well, so far I've been delighted with the response to my SUMO book. It seems the messages that I've sought to communicate have struck a chord with thousands of people. What has thrilled me has been the range of people who have found the book helpful. One woman told me how her 82-year-old mother had read it (I would have loved to have been present when this lady received a book from her daughter entitled *SUMO – Shut Up, Move On*) and how her mother-in-law remarked that she wished she had read it when she was 20. Equally, I heard recently from the Director General of the Confederation of British Industry who, having read the book, wanted additional copies to give to some friends and colleagues. He felt that the SUMO ethos was essential for business success.

Although delighted at the response to the book in terms of feedback and sales, I believe personally that the SUMO message needs to spread further. I feel like a football manager whose team has won their opening three matches of the season ... it's a great start, but there's still a long way to go.

I'm immensely grateful for all the people who've contacted me as a result of reading SUMO. Within the first two weeks of the book's publication, I became wracked with self doubt as to whether anyone would find the book helpful. The following comments, from what were at the time total strangers, gradually helped to replace this tide of uncertainty with a sense of great privilege and personal satisfaction that SUMO was indeed beginning to make a difference.

Paul McGee
The SUMO Guy
January 2006

Feedback on the book

Hi Paul, a colleague of mine suggested I read your SUMO book as they wanted to introduce your SUMO principles into the workplace. To be honest, I'm a little sceptical of some of these self-help books, particularly when I knew it was written by a motivational speaker! Well I stand corrected. Having read the book and heard you speak, I'm now a fully signed up convert. Your SUMO principles make a lot of common sense and are written in a way that is easy to grasp and apply to every aspect of life.

Adam Smith,
Director, jjFox

Dear Paul,
Just wanted you to know that I found your SUMO book both stimulating and instructive. The world of business moves on at such a pace that I believe the SUMO ethos is an essential part of the business persons DNA.

Sir Digby Jones,
Director-General, CBI

Paul,
I was made redundant on Friday. It was a dull but well paid job – I wallowed (for half a day).

Then, still feeling angry and let down, on my way home, I bought your book in Heathrow Airport and read it from cover to cover while waiting for my flight. I have always been the type of person to see the opportunities when faced with adversity, but your book has given me the insight, courage and determination to pursue my dream career. Thank you!

Nikki Ritchie

Dear Paul,

I recently finished your SUMO book and loved it. I read if looking for better ways to motivate the kids I work with … having finished it, I'm the one who was motivated. I've seen the damage we can do to ourselves when we are trapped by our behaviour and past problems. Your SUMO concepts offer an achievable process for overcoming the restrictions of our past.

Eric O'Halleran

Hi Paul,

Loved the book! Was able to pick it up and read it in a day. Got into trouble with my wife though, when I started quoting from it – she's been telling me much of the same stuff over the past 27 years together!

Brian Bennet,
Communications Director, UCB Radio

Paul,

I'm an avid SUMO supporter! Our senior management team were recently given your book and I immediately embraced the ideas/concepts. I'm now running a programme for 'budding' leaders of the company and they have each received a copy of SUMO. I've even developed a short quiz based on your book and have requested that over the next month, they specifically look for ways in which the SUMO principles will help them in the working/personal lives.

Rose Hurley

Hi Paul,

Just want you to know what a huge difference your SUMO book has made to my life. I strive to listen to my Inner Coach now and I truly feel positive and good about myself and my life. I have left the demons and mistakes of the past where they belong (in the past) and I have moved on to living the life I want and deserve. Thank you and keep up the good work.

Carol Chalmers-Hunt

Paul,

Just a quick note to say how much I enjoyed your book. Clients and colleagues (I bought several copies) have found the book to be motivational and entertaining. I particularly loved your

personal stories which brought the book alive
and made it so easy to read.

Helen Ralston,
Director, Personnel Dynamics

Hi Paul,

I just wanted to congratulate you on your SUMO
book. It was a great read and by far and away the
best in the self-help category that I have read
recently. I coach people for a living and having
read a lot of these types of books, believe many
fail because they are too abstract or difficult to
put into practice. Your book however, is full of
practical things you can do straight away to start
to make a difference. I particularly liked the
'Ditch Doris Day' chapter.

Rob Parker

Paul,

Reading your book has totally changed the way I
think and see things. After going through a lot of
challenging life experiences the book has helped
me to move on and become a happier person
within myself.

David Higgs,
Special Needs Teacher

Hi Paul,

Having recently read your SUMO book, I decided to buy a copy for each member of staff. I've found it easy to read, humorous and above all, practical in the solutions it provides to meet the everyday challenges of life! Thank you.

Beverley Owen, Head Teacher

'Hi Paul. Every now and then you pick up a book which really hits the mark. SUMO is just such a book; extremely thought provoking and humorous. It's really had a valuable impact on the way I think and act and I will continue to SUMO! Many thanks.

Phillip Sefton,
Vice President Commercial Operations Europe
& International, Qiagen Ltd

Acknowledgements

I've written several books. None however has seen me draw upon the wisdom and support of so many people as this one. I am grateful to Roy Sheppard, who first suggested I write about my SUMO philosophy, and to Steve McDermott for all his encouragement and advice in finding a publisher. As for my three Wise Men; Paul Sandham, Tom Palmer and David Broster, your comments regarding the content and style of this book were invaluable.

I was asked recently who inspires me? Many people do. Paul Scanlon, your words helped me raise my game and provoked me to dream big and take action. I'm humbled by the incredible work you and your team are doing in Bradford, a place I see as my second home. As for my friends at the Professional Speakers Association, life is richer for knowing you all. Thanks also to Commander Kate, because your energy, initiative and creativity has been so vital in helping me to move on in my business. Dave Clifford, you've shared my highs and lows as a Bradford City fan, and for that, I salute you!

The Capstone team have been great to work with. I feel privileged to have found a publisher who shares my passion for self-development and who has a willingness to be creative in how these important truths are communicated.

And finally to my family. Your unwavering support sustains me. Helen, my wife, business partner and best mate, you continue to be my rock. Matthew and Ruth, I want you both to know that no father could be more proud of their children than I am of you. It's an honour to be your Dad (just remember who is in charge of the TV remote control – and it's not you!).

Paul McGee 2005

Introduction

'You don't have to be ill to get better'
Eric Berne

I spent 13 years at school. I learnt a lot. I learnt about algebra, how to use a Bunsen burner, how bad I am at woodwork, a few things about dinosaurs and the joys of life under the Romans. On reflection though, I don't feel I learnt much about life and how to make the most of it. I explored the inner workings of a frog, but I never learnt about how to understand myself and other people. I learnt to stand up when a teacher came into the room and to hand in my homework on time if I wanted to avoid detention, but I wasn't taught how to set goals, manage my emotions or how to handle conflict. For me, school prepared me for exams. It didn't prepare me for life. I appreciate a lot has probably changed in education now, but that was my experience.

If you asked me 12 years ago, 'would you like your life to be a brilliant and wonderful experience both for you and those around you?', I would have answered a resounding 'yes'. However, if you then asked me how I intended to make this happen, I would probably have waffled on for several minutes before coming to the conclusion 'I'm not so sure'. But I've learnt a lot over the last few years. My answer now would be very different.

Over these next six chapters, you will get to hear what my answers are. They are based on over ten years studying psychology, running my own business and more importantly based on my observations and conversations with tens of thousands of people. My job as a professional speaker and my experience of running workshops on subjects related to 'people, motivation and communication' has given me a fascinating insight into what does and doesn't work in people's lives. My work has taken me from Tanzania to Todmorden, from Hong Kong to Halifax, from India to Islington and from Malaysia to Manchester. Whatever the country, whatever the culture, I learnt this – people are basically the same. They have similar hopes, dreams and challenges. They want to improve their lives, be happy and create a better future for their children. Of course there are differences, but if you dig beneath the surface, you find overwhelming similarities.

Why SUMO?

A few years ago I came across the phrase SUMO. I don't recall who said it but I do remember what it stood for – **S**hut **U**p, **M**ove **O**n. To some people this seems like a rather aggressive statement, but let me explain what I mean when I say 'Shut Up, Move On'. Firstly, I am not suggesting people simply need to 'get over it' or 'pull themselves together' (although there may be occasions when both these responses are necessary). Neither does it mean 'forgive and forget' or 'just ignore reality and get on with life'. SUMO for me captures the essence of what I believe are the key truths around success and fulfilment. Let me elaborate.

When I was a child I learnt the Green Cross Code. It was a code intended to keep children safe when crossing the road. I learnt the phrase 'Stop, Look and Listen'. When I use the words 'Shut Up', I am encouraging people to *stop* what they're doing, take some time out and *look* at their lives and reflect on how they are thinking and behaving. I want people to *listen*. Yes, be prepared to listen to others but, more importantly, listen to yourself. Go beyond the noise-filled, activity-driven, fast-paced existence of daily life and spend some time alone with your own thoughts. 'Shut Up' also means 'let go'. As you read this book, there may be views and opinions you have about life that you have clung onto simply through habit. My goal is to challenge you to consider whether your outlook on life is helping or hindering you.

The '*Move On*' part of SUMO is saying a number of things. It is meant as an encouragement that whatever your past experiences, your future doesn't have to be the same. Tomorrow can be different from today if that's what you want. *Move On* is asking you to look at your future, to see the possibilities that lie ahead, rather than be stuck in the reality of your current circumstances. It's a call to take action, to do something. It's a challenge not to 'think on' but *Move On*' and we'll look at ways to make that happen.

The phrase SUMO now underpins my personal philosophy on how to make the most of life. It is a challenging phrase, but it's also one that is meant to encourage and inspire you both in your work and personal life. Hopefully it's a phrase you will always remember.

Let me explain my approach in writing this book. Firstly, I have aimed to make the concepts I write about memorable. For instance, I'm convinced there is not a book in the world that has the concept 'Ditch Doris Day'. I have also included sections called 'The personal stuff'. It's not compulsory that you read these sections, but I believe they bring life – and colour and context – to what we're exploring. They also reveal my own struggles and occasional successes as I wrestle with applying these ideas to my own life.

To help you engage further with the material, I ask a number of questions. Your experience of this book will be richer and more revealing and rewarding when you spend some time, however briefly, chewing over your answers.

Finally, although you might not notice, I have tried to add some humour. The ideas we look at are very important, but that doesn't mean we cannot have the occasional smile.

Enjoy

Paul McGee

Change Your T-shirt

Let me start by asking you the same two questions I ask people when I am running a workshop or speaking at a conference. Firstly, 'Do you drive a car?' And secondly, 'Did you get yourself dressed this morning?' If you answered yes to either question you'll relate to the following fact – *much of what we do in life we do without consciously thinking about it.* Ever had the experience of taking a familiar car journey and suddenly finding yourself at your destination and wondering 'How did I get here?' Or find yourself driving on the motorway and asking yourself 'What happened to those last ten miles?' When you got dressed this morning, did you consciously decide in what order to get dressed? Did you weigh up the pros and cons of which shoe to put on first? If not, then you probably identify with the concept I call 'auto-pilot syndrome'.

We are about to go on a journey. Except on this journey I want you to be very conscious of where you are going and how you get there. To do so, your first step in the SUMO process is to ensure that you take time out, off auto-pilot, and honestly assess how you have been living your life so far. To help you do this, here are three questions to consider.

1   Which person has the biggest influence on your life?

2   Who deserves the most credit for where you currently find yourself in life?

3   Whose advice and opinions do you tend to always act upon?

Let me share with you my answers. (Although I have to confess they would not always have been my response.)

1   Which person has the biggest influence on your life? *I do.*

2   Who deserves the most credit for where you currently find yourself in life? *I do.*

3   Whose advice and opinions do you tend to always act upon? *My own.*

How do they match yours? I admit there are many people who have influenced my life and who deserve credit for how they have helped me. And I have listened to the advice and opinions of others; but ultimately, the biggest single factor that determines where you and I currently find ourselves in life is 'you'.

> **SUMO wisdom**
>
> If you want to know who is most responsible for where you are in life, take a look in the mirror.

Here is the challenge. We live in a climate and culture where this outlook is not always encouraged. How comfortable do you feel about standing up and saying 'I take full responsibility for my life?' Let's explore why many people would not only feel uncomfortable saying that statement, they would also disagree with it. I call it the BSE crisis.

The great BSE crisis

I meet individuals who believe that their current circumstances in life have:

1   Nothing to do with the previous decisions they have made.

2   Nothing to do with the actions they have taken.

3   Nothing to do with the attitudes they have adopted.

Apart from that, they take full responsibility for everything.

If life is not as they would want it, they can quickly play their *BSE* card – *B*lame *S*omeone *E*lse. 'I mean, what can I do?' they ask, 'It's not my fault. Someone else is to blame.'

Not only do they carry their own personal BSE card, they also tend to wear a particular T-shirt. Confused? Let me explain.

Imagine for a moment that how you felt or what you believed about yourself was written on your T-shirt. Some T-shirts may have the phrase 'I am confident' or 'I feel good about myself'; whilst others may have 'I lack self-belief' or 'I don't like people' (I have met a few of those). BSE card carriers though, wear one with the message – '*Victim*'. Wearers of this T-shirt tend to think, say and believe the following:

> *'This is my life and I must grin and bear it.'*
> *'It's not my fault.'*
> *'Life is not fair.'*
> *'I've never been lucky.'*
> *'I blame the government/my parents/the traffic/my boss/my teachers/my kids.'*

'I cannot really change or influence my situation.'
'I'm not capable.'
'I'm not confident.'
'I'm not good enough.'

SUMO wisdom

When a group of victim T-shirt wearers get together they hold a 'blame storming' session.

The personal stuff

Have I ever worn the T-shirt? You bet. I failed my Geography 'A' Level and blamed the teachers, until someone pointed out that not every pupil in the class had failed.

In my early days of business I blamed the economy for my lack of success. Things were not buoyant when I began, but it was easier to use the excuse of outside factors than to take a look at my own actions and decisions.

More recently I failed to secure a place as a main speaker at a large sales conference. I had put a great deal of time and effort into persuading the organizers that I was the ideal speaker for this high profile event. When the 'no thanks' news came through I was gutted, particularly when I found out who had been chosen instead of me. I muttered to myself 'That's not fair ... I'm a far better speaker than him'. It took several hours before I realized that I was wearing the Victim T-shirt.

So why wear the T-shirt in the first place?

Here are four reasons why we might be tempted to wear the Victim T-shirt:

Reason 1
You feel you have no other choice. 'That's just the way it is, there's nothing I can do' is the mantra of people who play the victim role. You can adopt a fatalistic approach to life and to the inevitability of being the victim.

Reason 2
Low self-esteem and poor self-image. Either of these factors can distort your view of how you see a situation. Your esteem and self-image can be affected by 'life events' and you are more vulnerable to seeing them damaged when you have experienced a major change such as a divorce, redundancy or an illness. Such events can knock your self-confidence, which in turn affects how you think and feel about yourself.

Reason 3
It's become a habit. Some people have been putting on the T-shirt so regularly, they now wear it without even being conscious of the fact. Their wardrobe consists of a whole range of styles and colours of Victim T-shirts. One to suit any occasion.

Reason 4
People actually enjoy wearing it. My research reveals that wearing the Victim T-shirt can bring people many perceived benefits:

• People feel sorry for you and give you more attention.

• It can increase your own feeling of self-importance.

• It is a good excuse for not being able to achieve other things (I would have been able to achieve X if only Y had been more supportive).

• Blaming others frees you from the responsibility of taking charge of your own life.

Points to ponder

It's not easy to admit that you have worn the T-shirt. Maybe you haven't; but if you have, what has been your reason? Can you identify people you know who wear the T-shirt? What in your view motivates them to wear one?

The personal stuff

When I became ill with chronic fatigue syndrome I went from a high-flying management position to invalidity benefit. Life did not seem very fair and for a while I wore the Victim T-shirt. I used to queue up to collect my benefit on the same day pensioners got theirs. I was twenty-four years old. Talking about the weather and the price of baked beans became part of my everyday conversation and did little to make me feel better about myself. I eventually decided that I needed to excuse myself from the pity party and focus on what was still good about my life. I was surprised how much I found. For instance, I realized what an incredible wife I had and how fortunate I was to have so many supportive friends. We still had our own home and I found time to join a creative writing group. We even managed the occasional weekend away, courtesy of someone else's generosity.

People are not always conscious they are wearing the T-shirt. You might not be. Let's explore some characters I have come across on my travels, which may help you spot the signs more clearly.

Victim T-shirt wearers on parade

First let's meet Colin, who is in his early thirties and always has a reason for why he can never remain in a job for longer than three months. He claims he is the victim of office politics; a boss who feels threatened by him, jealousy amongst fellow co-workers and finally, some plot by head office to make his life so unbearable he has no choice other than to resign. Colin is the master of conspiracy theories. On no occasion that I know of has he ever admitted that *he* might have something to do with losing his job.

Dave had been made redundant. He spent months harassing an organization for not appointing him to a position that in his words 'I was clearly right for'. During this time, he failed to apply for any other job until he dealt with what he saw as discrimination. (He did not specify on what grounds he was being discriminated against.) Rather than believe someone else had been more suited to the position, he chose to be the victim. Sometimes people *are* discriminated against and it is right for them to fight for justice. But on other occasions, discrimination is not the reason for people's lack of success – *they* are.

Several months ago I was coaching Lucy, who believed that success was a matter of luck and that she was not lucky. 'It's all about being in the right place at the right time,' she protested, 'and I never am'. Rather than identify and develop her skills and abilities, she chose to believe that life would only get better when she got her big break. Her 'victim mentality' verged on paranoia when she even blamed her accent. 'People think I'm posh and are threatened by me … particularly northerners.' (As a northerner myself I had to smile at such a comment.)

Finally Brian, an office worker I met on one of my courses, seemed to be full of regrets. 'I could really have made something of my life if it had not been for my elderly mother. She has been ill for over 20 years and I have had to look after her. Opportunities have passed me by, including marriage. But what else could I do?' Well, what could he have done? Perhaps if he had seen himself as less of a victim of his domestic circumstances, his life could have been very different. Having a sick or elderly mother does not automatically require a person to remain single. Brian thought it did.

SUMO wisdom

Taking personal responsibility frees you from the trap of blaming, complaining and resenting.

Points to ponder

Where are you most likely to wear the Victim T-shirt – at home or at work?

The consequences of wearing the Victim T-shirt

What do Colin, Dave, Lucy and Brian have in common? Simple – wearing the Victim T-shirt has consequences on your life. For them, these include:

• A failure to fulfil their potential.

• Missing out on opportunities because they were too busy feeling sorry for themselves to spot them.

- Other people failing to benefit from their talents.

- Feelings of regret because of what might have been.

- Stagnating, rather than growing as a people.

Points to ponder

You may have worn the Victim T-shirt regularly, or just on the odd occasion. But when you have, what have been the consequences both to you and those around you? What about the people you know who wear one? What has happened in their lives as a result?

Your choices are significant.
What you do affects who you are
and where you end up.

SUMO wisdom

Having explored the consequences of wearing the Victim T-shirt, you may decide you want to stop wearing one. I want to examine why changing it can be difficult. There are three reasons.

Removing your T-shirt means changing your status quo

You and I are creatures of habit. Living a life where we do not take responsibility for our actions and where we can blame others for our circumstances is convenient. It becomes a part of our normal way of living. It's what we are familiar with. To change means to move out of our self-created comfort zone. To some people, that is neither appealing or easy to do.

SUMO wisdom

When you wear the victim T-shirt, you become a passenger in your life and allow circumstances and other people to determine your direction.

Removing your T-shirt means going against the current fashion

In the past, when people had accidents, we saw it as part of everyday life and most people were usually prepared to accept some, if not all, the responsibility. Not any more. Our minds are bombarded with messages such as 'Where there's blame, there's a claim' (and in some cases that is appropriate). But we are now encouraged by some parts of society to feel like victims who are powerless to help ourselves. Blame your teachers, blame your parents, blame the government.

Blame anyone but yourself. We are told we are victims of stress, long hours and unsafe food. Seeds of victim mentality are sown when we are asked questions such as 'Have you felt stressed in the last month?' or 'Have you ever experienced bullying at work?' (Clearly some people do genuinely face such challenging situations, but tackling the problem whilst wearing a Victim T-shirt will not help).

> Some people have become very aware of their rights, but less aware of their responsibilities.

SUMO wisdom

Removing your T-shirt requires courage

It can be uncomfortable to admit to yourself that you have been wearing a Victim T-shirt. This is even harder to do if you feel you are a genuine victim. So let me be clear. *I do believe* there are innocent victims in life who could justifiably wear the T-shirt. However, some genuine victims choose not to. They decide not to allow events or circumstances to define their identity. Why? Without exception, the people I have met who have been able to move on have done so because they hold on to the following belief:

SUMO wisdom

I am not always responsible for what happens to me, but I am responsible for how I choose to respond.

The personal stuff

In March 1993 my wife Helen and I went out for our regular Saturday morning shop. My desire to be back to watch a football programme meant we left town earlier than Helen would have hoped. As we drove out of the town centre a bomb exploded. It killed two young children. Helen, who was eight months pregnant at the time, had walked past the bin where the bomb was planted minutes before it detonated. Those families who lost their sons that day were genuine innocent victims. I met the father of one of those children recently. Remarkably he seemed to possess no enduring bitterness and appeared to adopt the following attitude.

SUMO wisdom

Even if you are a genuine victim, ultimately you need to learn how to become a survivor.

On a lighter note – during one of my presentations, I produced a large yellow T-shirt with the word *Victim* emblazoned across the front. I was making the point that we need to get rid of this type of T-shirt. At the end of my talk a man approached me wondering if I sold Victim T-shirts. He knew plenty of people where he worked who he could sell them to. In case you are wondering, I don't sell Victim T-shirts.

> **Points to ponder**
>
> What's holding you back from removing your Victim T-shirt?

So we know some of the reasons why we wear the T-shirt and why it can be difficult to change. But if you want to change it, *how* do you go about it?

How to change your T-shirt

First of all you must decide you want to. Then you need to choose a new one with a different message. The message I suggest is *SUMO*. When you wear this T-shirt, you are deciding to *S*hut *U*p being a victim and *M*oving *O*n to taking responsibility. If you want things to be different in your life, you have to make different choices and take different actions. The rest of the book will show you how to do this, but you can make an immediate start by learning to 'mind your language'. We need to remove victim language from what we say and what we think and replace it with SUMO sayings. Let me give you some examples.

Avoid victim language Language	Replace with SUMO
Life is not fair what can I do?	I am unhappy about that,
This is just the way I am	How can I improve?
There's nothing I can do can do	There's always something I
It's impossible	Let's find a way
Who is to blame? forward?	How can we move
I am a victim	I am a survivor

The personal stuff

As I review the list, I admit that my language has not always been overflowing with SUMO sayings. In the past I have given up too easily because 'There's nothing I can do'; rather than choose the more empowering statement 'There's always something I can do'. I have found it interesting how closed my mind has become to exploring further possibilities when I have adopted the attitude 'It's impossible'. As soon as I put on the Victim T-shirt, it's as if the solution-seeking part of my brain goes into temporary shut-down mode. When you wear the T-shirt you stop looking at how to help yourself.

Points to ponder

Which victim sayings have you found yourself using? Choose an example of a SUMO saying that you are going to be more conscious of using in the next week.

In a nutshell

Let me be really clear about what changing your T-shirt does and does not mean. To do so I am going to answer the two most common questions that people pose when we're exploring this topic.

1   *Does removing the Victim T-shirt mean I have to accept full responsibility for everything that has happened to me even when it's not my fault?* No. Removing the T-shirt simply means you accept responsibility for how you choose to respond to an event. You do not necessarily have to blame yourself for what has happened, but

you should accept responsibility for how to move forward.

2 *But what if I do believe I have been unfairly treated or discriminated against? Are you suggesting I simply 'get over it' and stop making a fuss?* Absolutely and categorically not. The key is not to remain helpless. You may have been a 'victim' but you must see yourself as a survivor. You must assert yourself when necessary and do all you can to challenge inappropriate actions by an individual or organization.

The message from this chapter is that some people, consciously or unconsciously, habitually wear the Victim T-shirt. In doing so, they abdicate responsibility for their lives. Removing the T-shirt is an indication that no matter what life has given us so far or will give us in the future, we take control of our response. If you want your life to get better, you'll never be able to achieve it until you remove your T-shirt. Change does not happen when circumstances improve; change happens when *you* decide to improve your circumstances.

Get off auto-pilot and take back the controls of your life.

SUMO
wisdom

SUMO summary

- Shut *Up* the 'auto-pilot syndrome' and Move On to self-awareness.
- Shut *Up* 'Blaming Someone Else' and Move On to personal responsibility.
- Shut *Up* missed opportunities, regret and stagnation. Move On to fulfilling your potential, using your talents and growing as a person.
- Shut *Up* being the passenger; Move On to being in the driving seat of your life.
- Shut *Up* speaking 'victim' language; Move On to speaking SUMO language.
- Shut *Up* wishing your life would get better; Move On to making it so.

Chapter 2

Develop Fruity

Thinking

I love quotes. Perhaps my favourite is one I made up (humility always was my strong point). It goes as follows:

'The most important person
you will ever talk to is yourself.'

In the first chapter we explored how we can hinder our lives by talking to ourselves and others in victim language. Talking to yourself (at least silently) is generally referred to as thinking. In this second SUMO principle we are going to explore how we think. Thinking is a little like breathing – most of the time we are not aware we are doing it. People do not wake up in the morning and say 'I think I will breathe today', and likewise, neither do they pay much attention to how they think.

So why is it so important? What is the connection between my thinking and the results I am experiencing in my life? The answer lies in the fact that the way we think, i.e. talk to ourselves in our head, significantly impacts upon what we do in our actions, and it is our actions that determine the results we achieve in life.

The TEAR model

Imagine you have been asked by a work colleague to make a presentation to their department about the work you do. Your immediate thought is, 'I hate making presentations, I always go to pieces'. You feel intimidated by the prospect and decline the request by stating you have too many other commitments at present. The result? You still fear presentations and you miss out on the opportunity of helping a colleague. You just went through the TEAR process:

*T*hinking → *E*motions (or feelings) → *A*ctions (or behaviour) → *R*esults (or outcomes)

William James, one of the pioneers of modern psychology, said 'You can change your life by changing your attitude'. Quite simply, when you *think* differently, you *feel* differently, *behave* differently and ultimately *achieve* different results. Suppose when you were asked to do the presentation, you thought 'I'll give it a try ... they wouldn't have asked me if they didn't feel I could do it'. You might not feel confident, but neither are you gripped by fear. You take action by preparing and then delivering your presentation. You get a different result and outcome because you changed how you thought about the situation.

SUMO wisdom

Reflecting on how we think is one of the most powerful ways we can take more control over our lives.

What influences your thinking?

How you view your life, yourself and other people is influenced by many factors. Let us examine four of them.

1 Your background influences your thinking

A leading British entrepreneur records in his biography how, as a youngster, his mother would often tell him the following: 'Dare to be different'; 'Be prepared to rock the boat'; 'It's OK to make mistakes as long as you learn from them'; 'Life is not a rehearsal'; 'Never forget – no one is any better or worse than you'. Brought up in that environment, it is not surprising that this person became a risk taker, a visionary leader and a person who, despite setbacks, always bounced back. Contrast that with a delegate on my course who told me recently that his father's advice on how to succeed in life was 'Always wear navy and keep a low profile'.

The most important message you receive as you grow up is the one that influences how you see yourself. Messages that affirm you for who you are, as opposed to for what you do, will help you develop a healthy sense of personal identity. Equally, a bombardment of messages that remind you of your inadequacies and failings will help sow the seeds of low self-esteem.

> Be careful what you say to children.
> If they hear it often enough,
> they begin to believe it.

SUMO wisdom

2. Your previous experiences influence your thinking
Have you ever had to give a talk in public? Imagine (if you need to) that you have, and your input was such that most of the audience were cured of their insomnia. It would be understandable that you do not rush to do another one.

Or maybe when you took a risk or tried something different, you did not get the outcome you were expecting. It is likely that you will be more cautious in the future. Perhaps the last time you went to a restaurant you received excellent service and you are eager to return. *Whatever your previous experiences have been, they influence your attitude and your expectations.* This also relates to when we meet people, and is why aiming to create a positive first impression is so important. Our brief encounters with people can create attitudes that last a lifetime.

3   The company you keep influences your thinking
The 1970s British comedy series *Dad's Army* starred a Scottish character called Frazer. When not in the Home Guard, he worked in a funeral parlour. It suited his personality. Whenever there was a set of circumstances or a situation that could be described as challenging, Frazer would cry 'We're dooooooomed!' Watching Frazer was amusing, but working with a 'Frazer-type character' is not. Someone who exaggerates problems and can always pinpoint the negative in a situation does not help cultivate a positive way of thinking in those around them.

SUMO wisdom

Beware of BMWs.
People who spend their lives
Bitching, Moaning and Whinging.

4 The media influences your thinking

What have you read in the last week? A newspaper? A magazine? Which television programmes have you watched, or radio shows have you listened to? Although we may watch a programme or read a magazine purely for entertainment, or in order to 'chill out', continual exposure to the media subtly influences our outlook on life.

Without the media, where would fashion be? Where would celebrities be? Where would politics be? There is nothing inherently wrong with the media, but we need to be aware of how it shapes our thinking, particularly in relation to how we see ourselves. The obsession in some parts of the media with the appearance of supermodels and celebrities can cause young people in particular to feel dissatisfied with their own appearance and can affect what they think of themselves.

The personal stuff

While I was working with a group of people who had been made redundant, I explained how their view that 'there are no jobs' was a distorted one. I showed them a regional newspaper I had been reading that included a story on their *front page* about a pensioner who dropped a frozen turkey on her foot. Fortunately, after her foot was X-rayed she was given the all clear by the hospital and discharged. Tucked away in the same paper on page three was a story about 800 new jobs being created in the area. I then showed them another paper where the news of a factory closing down was on the front page. These people's view of the job market was influenced by what the media chose to highlight. Negative news and mindless trivia dominated the front pages. The positive stories were harder to find.

So our thoughts, beliefs and attitudes are influenced by several factors. They shape our lives whether we are aware of them or not. The key to all this is self-awareness. However, whilst it is important to recognize the influence of various external factors, be careful you don't start to slip on the Victim T-shirt, i.e. 'I think negatively because of how my parents brought me up', or 'My wife insists we watch medical dramas where there's never a happy ending.' We still need to take personal responsibility for our thinking despite those external influences.

Points to ponder

Consider how your upbringing and background has influenced how you see yourself. What messages about yourself do you remember hearing as a child? Were they mainly positive or negative ones? Think about your circle of friends. How do they influence your thinking? Be aware when you next read a paper or watch a television programme how they are influencing your view of the world.

We highlighted earlier, through the TEAR model, (*T*hinking, *E*motions, *A*ctions, *R*esults) the importance of our thinking. Let's examine in more detail how certain types of thinking patterns can hinder our ability to be successful. I refer to these thinking patterns as 'faulty thinking'.

Four types of faulty thinking

The first type of faulty thinking ...the Inner Critic

This is the voice inside your head that highlights your weaknesses and undermines your confidence. It is not the voice of encouragement to do better, it is the voice of condemnation. You make a mistake on Tuesday and ten days (or ten years) later you are still beating yourself up about it. The need to *S*hut *U*p criticizing yourself is great, but people fail to *M*ove *O*n. In extreme cases, you are beating yourself up about events and actions that happened years ago. Driven perhaps by the mistaken belief that 'I must be perfect', or 'It is wrong to make mistakes', the Inner Critic can help demolish your fragile walls of confidence.

SUMO wisdom

Remember, each of us is complex.
None of us is perfect.
Mistakes happen.
Move On.

The Inner Critic takes root in our lives from early childhood, and is fed and watered by the four factors we have just explored:

1   Your personal background

2   Your previous experiences

3   The company you keep

4   The media.

The personal stuff

I recently worked in a local school with a group of 11–12 year olds. I started to explore the 'Inner Critic' with them and help them to understand its destructive nature. In order to tackle it, I suggested that we needed to expose it. I split them up into small groups and asked them to write a list of sayings that they might hear from the Inner Critic. Deep down, I hoped they would struggle to come up with many. Within five minutes, they were asking for more paper.

The language of the Inner Critic includes

'I ought …'
'I must …'
'I should …'
'I'm always getting it wrong.'
'How could I have been so stupid?'

Sometimes the voice of the Inner Critic speaks as an internal third party. These are phrases I have regularly heard inside my own head:

'Why didn't you …'
'That's typical of you.'
'You always get that wrong.'

> *'Don't get ideas above your station.'*
> *'Do you honestly think people will want to hear that?'*

The emotional intensity behind what you say to yourself determines whether the impact of the Inner Critic is that of a common cold (annoying but not life-threatening) or pneumonia (much more serious with potentially damaging consequences).

SUMO wisdom

It's not simply what you say to yourself that matters. It's how you say it and how much you believe it that counts.

Silencing the Inner Critic, however, is not an abdication of your desire to improve or an abandonment of responsibility regarding a mistake made. Your ultimate goal is to become a coach to yourself and not allow past mistakes to make a prisoner of your potential.

We still need to have conversations with ourselves, but the voice we need to listen to is that of the *Inner Coach*. This voice has your best interests at heart. It is *for* you. The Inner Critic condemns you. The Inner Coach encourages you and inspires you to improve, and in a few pages' time you will learn how to tune in to this voice.

The personal stuff

My Inner Critic raises its head when I've made a mistake. It's skilled at allowing me to spend days, even weeks beating myself up over some things that were genuine mistakes. Some years ago I was best man at a wedding. Before the meal I, along with the bridal party, lined up to greet the guests before they sat down to eat. I noticed one woman wearing a maternity dress who looked like she was due to give birth in the very near future. My suspicions were confirmed when the groom commented 'Not long to your big day then?' 'No, only three weeks' she replied, 'and I can hardly wait'. When it was my turn to meet her I made momentary eye contact then looked at her bump and enquired 'What are you hoping for, a boy or a girl?' The silence was deafening. Then she leaned forward and replied, 'I get married in three weeks and I am not pregnant.' Cue the Inner Critic. I found it hard to forgive myself for causing such embarrassment. But I learned my lesson. I am so mindful now that even if I am in a maternity ward, I would be hesitant to make any comments – and with good reason. A friend of mine who knew a neighbour was due to give birth imminently, asked her, 'When are you due?' She replied, 'I gave birth two weeks ago'.

Points to ponder

Do you suffer from the Inner Critic? What phrases do you find your Inner Critic saying to you? In what situations do you find the Inner Critic speaks loudest? Does it happen more at work or at home?

The second type of faulty thinking ... the Broken Record

When we get stuck in a groove of thinking, we continually replay the same messages within our head. You could be in 'Broken Record Inner Critic' mode whereby you continually analyze and criticize your behaviour. Alternatively you might simply keep on talking to anyone and everyone about your unhappiness and dissatisfaction with your job, a person, or a situation. Stuck in this way of thinking, you churn over your thoughts but take no action to resolve your problem.

There may be times when the problems of your past don't need to be fixed or sorted — they need to be left behind.

SUMO wisdom

Points to ponder

What do you tend to moan about? Why? How long does your moaning last? Does it make you feel better? What effect does it have on you and other people?

The third type of faulty thinking ... the Martyr Syndrome

I know martyrs can be viewed as heroic and their actions taken as a sacrifice for a worthy cause. But when I use the term in this context I mean the sort of thinking that says the following:

'I am unworthy.'
'I must sacrifice my needs to serve others.'
'I don't deserve to be happy.'
'My views are less important than other people's.'

SUMO
wisdom

Suffering from the Martyr Syndrome is more a reflection of how you see yourself as opposed to your dedication to serve others.

The reasons for suffering this type of thinking have been covered in the previous chapter, 'Change Your T-shirt'. However, there is one cause we have yet to mention as to why martyrs wear 'Victim T-shirts'.

SUMO
wisdom

When I punish me, I am actually trying to punish you.
I play the martyr in the hope that it makes you feel guilty.

When you try and help a martyr who has been complaining about how unfair life is, and why it is always them that has the 'short end of the stick', they often refuse. It is difficult to continue playing the martyr when you accept help from others. Some people are actually at their happiest when they've got something to be miserable about.

Points to ponder

When have you played the Martyr? Does it happen most with family and friends or bosses and colleagues? When did you last ask for some help?

The fourth type of faulty thinking ... Trivial Pursuits

Another way of understanding this type of thinking is when we make mountains out of molehills (although we'll see in our final chapter when this is appropriate). People have the ability to get angry or upset over the most trivial issues. Relationships are ruined and people suffer from anxiety, often not because of something major, but due to something insignificant. Trivial Pursuits can have a snowball effect and distort your view of reality.

What you focus on magnifies.

SUMO wisdom

This inability to see things in perspective can result in a reaction or outburst that is completely disproportionate to the actual event. Sounds familiar? It does to me. This type of thinking can be closely allied to the others. You can be a 'Broken Record Inner Critic' about something quite trivial. And we may play the martyr because of some insignificant event. For example, let us say that at work some information was not passed on to you, and although it was of little relevance, your response is, 'No one ever tells me anything around here, I'm always the last to know'. Here is the key point. Your emotional energy can be exhausted due to trivial pursuits and your focus can be distracted from the really important issues in your life.

SUMO wisdom

Perhaps it's not the circumstances that need to change, but more your perspective of those circumstances.

Points to ponder

What are some of the trivial issues you allow yourself to get upset over? What are the consequences of your reaction? When do you get into Trivial Pursuits? At work? In the car? With your children? With your partner?

The personal stuff

I recently worked with an organization on a 'Succeeding Through Change' programme for managers and staff. What fascinated me was what constituted 'massive change' for some staff. One guy said, 'They've only gone and moved my desk' (it was still in the same office). Others complained that the coffee machine had moved to a different floor and they now had to climb the stairs in order to get a drink. From my own experience, I have been close to declaring war due to the fact that I often find toothbrushes in every room of the house except the bathroom.

Why slip into faulty thinking?

At times we all slip into faulty thinking and often for quite irrational reasons. So why do we do it? To understand this, it is helpful to understand how your brain works. Let me give you a helpful model.

How the brain works

If we were to take a cross-sectional view of your brain, we could divide it into three distinct sections.

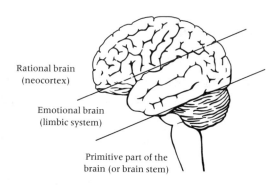

Rational brain
(neocortex)

Emotional brain
(limbic system)

Primitive part of the
brain (or brain stem)

1   **Rational brain.** Sometimes referred to as
    the neo cortex or 'higher brain'.

2   **Emotional brain.** This is part of the limbic
    system and is sometimes referred to as the
    'mid-brain'.

3   **Primitive brain.** Also known as the reptili-
    an brain or 'lower brain', it controls our fight
    or flight response, our desire for food and our
    sex drive.

So when we are feeling tired, hungry, anxious or
threatened, we are not feeling particularly rational.
In the heat of the moment, we may lash out physically or verbally, or run away from a situation in a
state of panic. This is our fight or flight response. We
react to a situation without first thinking through

our response. (This might explain the scenes in my household when I can't find my toothbrush.)

The upside of the primitive and emotional brain

However, to be driven by our emotional or primitive brain is not necessarily wrong; it is part of who we are as human beings. If everyone were completely rational about things in life, our world would lack passion, variety and excitement. Appreciating the highs only happens because we have experienced the lows. And being rational can sometimes be dangerous. If you are in a meeting room and a man-eating lion (who also has a taste for women) walks in, the rational response: 'How did that get in here and why isn't it wearing a visitor's badge?' will do little to save you. When it comes to matters of life and death, primitive brain wins every time. We don't have time to be rational; we must react instinctively.

Our emotional brain helps us to appreciate art, to be passionate about something and to engage creatively in an idea. People are moved to take action over an issue, not due to some rational urge, but because emotionally they feel compelled to do so.

The upside of the rational brain

Some of the problems and challenges we face in life are due to our inability to tap into our rational brain. Being rational can bring a fresh perspective and new insights to an issue. It helps us to utilize the problem-solving attributes of our higher brain. It can prevent us over-reacting to an event, and avoid saying and doing something that we later regret. By accessing our rational brain, we can discover an antidote to faulty thinking. It is a process I refer to as 'Developing Fruity Thinking'.

So how can we engage our rational brain?

The key to engaging your rational brain is to ask yourself questions. Questions are powerful. The quality of them determines the quality of your answers. To understand this more fully, let's explore for a moment how our amazing brain works.

The influence of your RAS

Your RAS (*Reticular Activating System*) is a part of your brain that filters information. Our brains are being continually bombarded with thousands of pieces of information from the environment around us. If we were to consciously take note of them all, we would experience brain overload. So your RAS acts like a filter and helps you to 'notice' information that is relevant, important, of interest or perhaps unusual.

I do a great deal of driving. Ask me which car is the most popular on the road and I would not be able to tell you. However, when I was thinking of getting myself a different type of car, I suddenly noticed that car everywhere. When my wife became pregnant, we immediately noticed how many other women were expecting babies. (Although because of my previous experience I couldn't always be sure and I certainly wouldn't ask when they were due.)

When we are experiencing faulty thinking, our brain seeks out information to support what we are thinking. If we believe we are always failing, then our RAS spots examples to reinforce that belief. Interestingly it also ignores the evidence that we were not looking for. For example, asking me to count how many BMW cars I see on the motorway means I ignore and fail to notice other makes of car.

Equally when I am looking for my failures, I ignore my successes. Questions such as 'Why am I so unlucky?' or 'Why does this always happen to me?' tune in your RAS to seek out information as to why you are not succeeding. *But when you change the question you change your focus.* Your RAS starts to notice 'things' it had previously been ignoring. So let's explore how to re-tune our RAS and tap into the benefits of using our rational brain.

The following seven questions have provided me with a way of moving on from the faulty thinking of the Inner Critic, the Broken Record, the Martyr Syndrome and Trivial Pursuits and into fruity thinking. They are the questions I use when I'm listening to the Inner Coach. With each question I have included its underlying message.

1 Where is this issue on a scale of 1—10?
Decide what is really important.

2 How important will this be in six months' time?
See the big picture. Get things in perspective.

3 Is my response appropriate and effective?
You choose your response.

4 How can I influence or improve the situation?
Identify your own resources to bring about change.

5 What can I learn from this?
Look for the learning in everything – even setbacks.

6   What will I do differently next time?
Learning brings change.

7   What can I find that's positive in this situation?
Searching for the positive opens our mind to new
possibilities.

There is nothing remarkable about the questions,
but it is the answers they lead to that can help
us succeed. They have become part of my 'life
tool kit' and one of the strategies I use to help
me tackle various challenges and situations that
I regularly face. (You can download a copy of the
seven questions by visiting www.TheSumoGuy.
com.)

If you are not happy with the
answers life is giving you,
then ask some different questions

**SUMO
wisdom**

So let's explore the importance of each question.
As we do, it would help if you had a particular
challenge or issue in mind. As we work through
the questions, see which will help you to see your
situation in a new light. The first three questions
are designed to help you *Shut Up*. To *Shut Up*
means to pause, to reflect and to listen. It means,
get off auto-pilot and stop reacting to a situation

like you always do. They are designed to provide perspective. When we are in emotional and primitive brain we tend to lose perspective.

1 Where is this issue on a scale of 1–10?

I am often asked, what do I mean by the scale of 1–10? For me 'one' on the scale means something insignificant and minor, whereas 'ten' represents a major issue, such as death, for example. Your scale is determined by your values. A scratch on my car is definitely a below-five event, whereas I appreciate for some people it is close to being a ten! Sometimes in the immediacy of the moment, I react to an event as if it is a nine; yet this question can quickly remind me it may only be a two. Where is your issue on the scale? How important and serious is it in relation to other areas of your life?

2 How important will this be in six months' time?

This is very similar to the first question. Again it is asking us to put things into perspective. It can serve as a reminder that what we are allowing to cause us great stress at the moment could actually be forgotten in six months' time. (Stop reading for a moment. Cast your mind back six months. Can you remember what was causing you stress at the time? Probably not, eh?) Is your issue something you may struggle to recall six months from now? If not, fine. At least you are gaining some perspective.

3 Is my response appropriate and effective?
What a great question to ask ourselves. This question allows you to consider whether or not your response will ultimately help or hinder the situation. A knee-jerk reaction that might seem reasonable at the time may seem very different a few hours or even a few minutes later. How effective and appropriate has your response been so far? If it is still an issue then do you need to change your response?

Sometimes it's good to take immediate action. But beware; there are times when if you strike whilst the iron is hot, people get burnt.

SUMO
wisdom

The next four questions are designed to help us to 'Move On' and to focus on how to achieve a different outcome.

4 How can I influence or improve the situation?
When we are under stress, our emotions have a habit of hijacking the problem-solving skills within our higher brain. Asking ourselves this question immediately helps us to focus on how

we can resolve the situation. It helps us *Shut Up* blaming circumstances and people for our situation and to *Move On* to identify ways we can help ourselves. Remember that learning to help ourselves may still involve the support of other people. How can you influence your situation? You may not be able to bring about a perfect outcome, but how can you improve things? Who could help you? What are your options?

The personal stuff

I once ran a workshop on interviewing skills for a group of office staff who were about to be made redundant. One woman remarked, 'I'll go to pieces if they ask me what my weaknesses are. I hate that question and just pray I'm not asked it.' 'What if they do?' I replied. 'Well, fingers crossed they don't or I'm in trouble.'

Hope is not a strategy. This woman clearly thought it was. By the end of the course, we had focused on what answers she could give if asked about her weaknesses. Common sense I know – but not always common practice.

5   What can I learn from this?

Life is always trying to teach us things. A great many people I talk with relate to having spent time beating themselves up over a mistake they've made. I have found a great antidote to my Inner Critic is this question. Rather than send myself on a guilt trip, can I use whatever has happened as an opportunity to learn? What is life trying to teach you through this issue?

6   What will I do differently next time?

If I repeat the same mistake, then I have not actually learnt anything. Real learning brings about change. Learn from it. Make changes. Move on. Regarding your issue, how will you deal with it differently next time? How will you change your approach?

7   What can I find that's positive in this situation?

In my work as a speaker, I realize this: sometimes it is not new ideas that people crave, it is the inspiration to implement the ideas they have. This question moves us away from what is wrong in a situation and directs our attention to what we can find that is positive. When we do so, we may identify possibilities we failed to see previously. We need inspiration to move forward. This question can provide it. What can you find that's positive in your situation?

The personal stuff

A couple of years ago, a potential new client e-mailed me. I had been recommended to them as someone who could speak to their staff on the subject of motivation. They were a high profile organization with an international reputation. To gain such a prestigious client would be a real coup for my business. We spoke on the phone and successfully agreed fees, dates and the content of my presentation. It only remained for some minor details to be ironed out before the event. I was thrilled. A few days later, having not received the confirmation promised, I e-mailed them a reminder. They replied instantly. It was not the news I wanted to hear. 'Due to circumstances, we are no longer able to proceed, but can I thank you for your interest in working with our organization.' I was fuming and felt tempted to put on my Victim T-shirt. In my anger and disappointment, I immediately set about responding to their e-mail. There were a number of issues I wanted to address.

1   How long had they known they no longer required my services? I had held the agreed date for several days and turned down another opportunity.
2   A phone call rather than hide behind a vague e-mail would have been appreciated.

3   As for their comment 'thank you for your inter-
     est in working with us as an organization'; well
     excuse me, but who contacted whom first?

As I typed the e-mail, I felt an increasing sense of
self-satisfaction. I would teach them to let me down
in such an unprofessional manner. Then in mid-sen-
tence, I stopped and thought *Is my response appropriate and effective?'* Well, it certainly felt appropriate, but was it going to be effective? If I pressed the
'Send' button, any opportunity of working with the
organization in the future would be zero. So what did
I do? Pressed delete and then did nothing for twenty-
four hours. Then when I re-read their e-mail I thought
about the fourth question to help me SUMO.

How can I influence or improve the situation?
My focus changed from feeling like the victim and
believing I had been treated unfairly, to tuning
in my RAS to identify another way forward. In a
calmer, more solution-focused state, I sent my response. Although not sure of the reason why my
services were no longer required, I suggested running a lunchtime session for staff for a reduced
fee and also gave them further options regarding
what other topics I could talk about. Within two
hours, they had booked me to speak. They had
their speaker and I had a new prestigious client.

Just as you do not cut the hedge with the lawn-mower, so it is also important to recognize that each question is appropriate in some situations but not in others. As you will see in the next chapter, sometimes people are not ready emotionally to ask themselves these questions. They are not a quick-fix magic solution. However, what they can do is cause us to take time to reflect and focus our mind in a more productive way.

SUMO wisdom

The quality of the solution can depend on the quality of the question.

Points to ponder

Which of the seven questions were most useful in helping you work through your issue? Choose two questions you want to be more conscious of using in the next few weeks.

In a nutshell

Faulty thinking is often based on the following false beliefs:

- *Inner Critic:* 'I lack value. My only worth comes through my performance and what other people think of me. When I fail to reach a particular standard I must punish myself.'

- *Broken Record:* 'Talking and thinking about something for long enough is an adequate substitute for taking action.'

- *Martyr Syndrome:* 'Life is what happens to me. I am not responsible for what happens; fate, luck and other people determine my destiny.'

- *Trivial Pursuits:* 'Urgency determines importance. That is how to prioritize. Ignore the big picture.'

The antidote to faulty thinking is fruity thinking. It comes when we listen to our Inner Coach and take a conscious grip of our thoughts. Fruity thinking is based on the following beliefs:

1   I am of worth because of who I am, not because of what I do.

2   I learn from the past but I do not remain rooted in it. I know when to let go and when to move on.

3   I am responsible. I have choices. No one else plays as big a role in determining my destiny as I do.

4   I choose to major on the majors. I am aware of the big picture and focus on what is important. I see things in perspective.

SUMO summary

- If you want different results in your life, change your thinking. *Thinking* → *Emotions* → *Actions* → *Results*
- Shut *Up* the auto-pilot and *Move On* to self-awareness. Our thinking is influenced by our background, previous experience, the company we keep and the media.
- Shut *Up* the Inner Critic and *Move On* to listening to the Inner Coach.
- Shut *Up* being a Broken Record and *Move On* to taking action.
- Shut *Up* the Martyr Syndrome and *Move On* to taking ownership of your life.
- Shut *Up* Trivial Pursuits and *Move On* to majoring on the majors.
- Shut *Up* being overly-dominated by your emotional and primitive brain and *Move On* to using your rational brain.
- Shut *Up* immediately reacting and *Move On* to choosing your response.
- Shut *Up* the questions that lead to faulty answers and *Move On* to fruity thinking.

Chapter 3

Hippo Time Is OK

Recently a delegate took me to one side and said, 'Paul, I enjoy what you're saying and I agree with it up to a point. But sometimes it isn't easy to SUMO. Sometimes I'm not ready to move on. Is that wrong?'

You may be thinking the same question. To answer it let me tell you about my friend Steve.

Steve was recounting how his favourite rugby league team had lost an important cup match. When he returned home his wife, who does not share his passion for rugby, said, 'Never mind, there's always next year.' At the time, this was the last thing Steve wanted to hear. 'I just wanted to wallow, to be left alone and to dwell on what might have been,' he told me. None of us want to hear some well-meaning person telling us to cheer up when we've just experienced a major setback or disappointment. Telling someone to SUMO might in some circumstances be both insensitive and unhelpful, particularly if what they have experienced is serious and significant. So what should we do?

When Steve used the term wallow, a picture of a hippopotamus wallowing in mud immediately sprang to mind. It was then that I realized that on occasions, before people can SUMO they may need to wallow – to have, as I call it, some *Hippo Time*. So when might you need Hippo Time?

When Hippo Time might be necessary

The need for Hippo Time will vary according to the person and their situation. But here are some events that may trigger a period of wallowing:

- Your partner dumps you

- You miss out on that promotion at work

- You are one number short of a big win on the lottery

- You miss your train or plane

- Your sports team loses an important match

- You fail to get the job you were interviewed for

- A publisher rejects your latest book proposal

- An event you were looking forward to is cancelled unexpectedly

- A friend lets you down in some way

- You discover your brand new conservatory has a structurally unsafe roof and the company who built it has gone out of business (I'll explain this one later)

- Your organization announces more changes and as a result you move departments

- Your house is broken into

- You lose or break something of sentimental value

- You are made redundant

- You're an England football fan and the game has gone to penalties.

Why not add two of your own events that have led to a legitimate time of wallowing?

Points to ponder

Which of the above has happened to you? How did you feel when it occurred? How long did those feelings last?

Why do we need Hippo Time?

To be simply told to *Shut Up, Move On* when any, or if you are really unlucky, all of the above has occurred is to deny reality. As human beings we are by nature emotional. A life without experiencing emotional highs and lows would be boring and bland. You are not a robot who can turn your emotions on and off at the flick of a switch. In order to move on, you need at times to acknowledge the emotions you are feeling. There will be occasions when, with the help of the seven questions we explored in Chapter 2, that we can SUMO in an instant. But let us be real here – there will be other occasions when we need to take a Hippo Time detour.

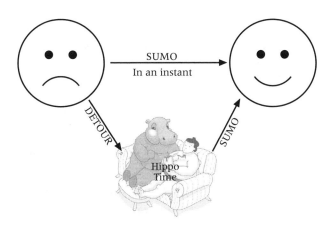

Hippo Time provides you with the opportunity to experience your emotional lows and to be honest about those feelings.

> **SUMO wisdom**
>
> When you deny the negative, you block the road to positive recovery.

Understanding our emotions

Sometimes we can become confused about our emotions. Is it wrong to cry? Should we always be happy? Let's get some clarity about our emotions.

Unhelpful beliefs about emotions	Helpful beliefs about emotions
Showing emotions makes you appear weak Men should never express their emotions Showing emotions embarrasses other people	Emotions are part of what makes us human Expressing emotions is a release valve for internal pressure No feeling is wrong, it is what we do with the feelings that counts.

Emotions are valid but they can also create confusion within us. Some people I know actually find value in keeping a 'feelings diary'. Rather than record what they did on a particular day, they record how they felt. Writing down our feelings may help us gain a greater insight into ourselves and also help us notice how our emotions vary from day to day.

Having Hippo Time can be extremely helpful. It can also be very unproductive. So how can you make the most of Hippo Time? Who is best to help you during this period and who should you avoid? How can you prevent yourself wallowing for too long? Here are some ground rules:

Top three tips for Hippo Time

Tip 1. Be careful who you talk to

The phrase *'a trouble shared is a trouble halved'* is an important principle, but it is not always appropriate. There are people who have the unique ability to make you feel worse after you have spoken to them. A friend of mine recalls how, having received a parking ticket, a colleague in his office told him he was the unluckiest person he had ever met. My friend was reminded of all the 'unlucky events' that had occurred to him over the last twelve months (many of which he had forgotten). When his colleague was told the cost of the ticket, the reply came, 'That's awful, just think what you could have done with that money'.

Some people, in seeking to help, encourage you to wear the Victim T-shirt and, metaphorically speaking, they are giving you more mud to wallow in. Also, avoid people who are only too keen to share advice before you have had a chance to vent, and who hijack your Hippo Time to recount all *their* worries and woes.

SUMO wisdom

Excuse me.
Whose Hippo Time is this?
I've started so I'll finish.

You may also want to avoid those 'I am positive but I have no grasp of reality' people. You lose your legs in an accident, and they smile sincerely and say, 'At least you've still got your arms.' You need to find someone who is prepared to actively listen, who allows you to talk and who doesn't feel obliged to offer advice.

Points to ponder

Who would you identify as the most appropriate person to have your Hippo Time with? Who would you avoid? Or do you prefer to have Hippo Time on your own?

Tip 2. Be careful how many people you talk to

Our temptation when asked the question, 'How are you?' or, 'How was your weekend?' is to answer honestly and comprehensively. After all, if we're in Hippo Time and someone asks the question, I'm entitled to give them an answer. Right? Wrong. There are two reasons why you have to be discerning about how many people you tell your troubles to.

Firstly, the more times you tell your story, the more you replay and re-live the negative experience and emotions associated with it. Distracted perhaps by a particular task or activity, you may actually feel fine until a colleague or neighbour enquires how you are. In that moment you have a choice. I am not suggesting that you 'put on a brave face' and deny that you are in Hippo Time. However, the question is this; does this person really want to know how you are, or are they simply making polite conversation? If it is the latter, give them your ten-second version of your story. If it is the former, then you may choose to tell the longer version, but only if you feel you want to.

SUMO wisdom

To re-tell is to re-live
and that is not always helpful.

Secondly – how can I put this nicely? Actually, I can't. So here goes: in my experience, around 80% of people who ask you how you are, are not particularly interested in your answer. Not only can it be unhelpful to go into replay mode about your troubles, but you may also be labelled a bore. So, for everyone's sake, beware how many people you share your Hippo Time with.

Points to ponder

How many people do you typically off-load your troubles to? Could that be considered too many?

SUMO wisdom

Sometimes it can be very helpful
to say about a particular topic,
'Let's not go there'.

Tip 3. Be careful how long your Hippo Time lasts
Some people can get used to wallowing in the mud. You may have been encouraged to lengthen your stay due to the attention you receive and wallowing can feel comfortable and comforting. But ultimately, spending too long in the mud of self-pity becomes unhelpful.

The longer you spend in Hippo Time, the harder it becomes to move on.

> **SUMO wisdom**

So how long should you spend in Hippo Time? Sorry to be vague, but it depends. When you start to reflect on the seven questions to develop fruity thinking, you are getting closer to moving on. However the length of time you spend wallowing depends on several factors:

- The seriousness of the issue

- The support you receive from others

- The amount of pay-offs you are receiving for staying in the mud (attention, sympathy, supply of Victim T-shirts, etc.)

- Your willingness to explore how to move on.

I am not here to give you guidelines on how long you need to wallow (e.g. broken relationship – four weeks; scratched car – three days; missing out on promotion – one week). But remember this:

SUMO wisdom

Hippo Time should never be a place of permanent residence.
Wallowing is temporary,
SUMO is forever.

The personal stuff

My wife and I had a beautiful conservatory built on the back of our house. There was hassle with the builders during construction, but we were delighted when it was eventually finished – until it started to leak. The leaks were fixed and again we started to enjoy this new addition to our home. Three months later, I discovered another small leak in the roof, and I rang the company to ask them to repair it. There was no reply. They had gone out of business. I finally tracked down another company prepared to tackle our problem roof, expecting a minor repair to cost a maximum of £100. To be then informed that the roof was in fact structurally unsafe and would cost several thousand pounds to rectify came as a nasty surprise. My wife and I were officially entering into Hippo Time. Did we tell lots of people? You bet. However, we quickly realized that every time we re-told what had happened, our anger increased. We stopped telling people and we felt better for it. Fortunately our insurance covered the cost of a new roof.

In order to move on, there is more to be gained by you looking forward than there is to you looking back. You need to be honest with yourself and ask this question: 'What is it costing me in terms of energy and opportunity to remain stuck in Hippo Time?' The answer to this question should help you decide on how long you spend wallowing.

Points to ponder

Think of an occasion when you were in Hippo Time. How long did you spend there? On reflection could you have moved on sooner? If so, what stopped you?

How do you help someone during Hippo Time?

It is probably helpful to start with what *not* to do.

- Don't fake-listen (i.e. pretend you are listening, when in fact you are wondering what to have for tea tonight, or whether your kids remembered to take their PE kit to school). The person talking will eventually realize you are not listening when they notice your eyes. They will be glazed over. You'll be having an OBE – an 'Out of Body Experience'. You know what I mean: the wheel's turning but the hamster's dead.

- Don't keep interrupting the other person with phrases such as, 'The same thing happened to me,' or, 'I know how you feel'. (How can you know how I feel? Is your conservatory structurally unsafe too?)

- Don't invade their Hippo Time and have yours instead. This is usually pre-empted with the comment, 'Well, you think that's bad – you should hear what happened to me today'. Your turn will come, just be patient.

- Don't keep using the phrase, 'That's awful' or 'That's terrible'. (Express some concern, but don't overdo it. What are you trying to do? Make them feel worse than they already are?)

> **The personal stuff**
>
> My wife Helen confesses there are perhaps cheaper and healthier ways to spend your time wallowing, but retail therapy and eating chocolate remain the most popular amongst her group of friends.

Here's what to do instead

- Work hard (and it can be hard work) to give the other person your full attention. If it's not a convenient time for you to listen, let them know when would be a good time.

- Allow the person to vent, i.e. get things off their chest.

- Allow the person to cry (if they need to) – no matter how uncomfortable it makes you feel.

- Use phrases such as, 'It's OK to be angry' or 'You seem very hurt by that'. (Use language you are comfortable with. I'm not suggesting you need to sound like a therapist).

- Give the other person space. Some people (particularly men) prefer to spend Hippo Time on their own. It would be helpful to say, 'Look, I appreciate you're upset. You know where I am if you need me', and then allow them time to themselves.

- When you feel it is appropriate, you might then use humour to diffuse the situation or put things into perspective. (Remember you need to be really careful about this, so if in doubt, avoid doing it).

Points to ponder

Think of whom you could help when they're in Hippo Time. Remember that you could hinder the experience depending on your response to them. Of the advice given on how to help people, which do you need to be most aware of?

The personal stuff

I, personally, like to go for a walk on my own when I'm wallowing. Although I admit a 112-mile walk was a bit extreme when Bradford City were relegated, but then I did have a lot of things to work through.

In a nutshell

Hippo Time is a valid place to be for some people before they can Shut Up, Move On. To deny and suppress our hurt and disappointment is unhealthy. However, spending too long in Hippo Time, especially with the wrong people, will not aid our recovery.

SUMO summary

- Before you can SUMO you may need to take a detour to Hippo Time.
- Remember: the more times you replay your story, the more you re-live it. Sometimes, we need to SUMO rather than re-tell.
- Sharing your Hippo Time with anyone and everyone is not appropriate; be choosy who you include in your Hippo Time. Shut Up telling every-

one your issues and Move On to people who will be more supportive.

- Be aware that the longer you spend in Hippo Time, the harder it is to Move On.
- Hippo Time is temporary. SUMO lasts a lifetime.
- When helping people in Hippo Time, Shut Up the fake listening, the interrupting and the 'awfulizing' and Move On to giving your full attention. Allow people time to vent, and be sensitive to the fact that they may prefer to be left alone.

Chapter 4

Remember

The Beachball

The first three SUMO principles have focused on increasing our personal self-awareness. They could be put under the heading 'Understanding Yourself'. This fourth SUMO success principle moves us on from our own inner world and helps us to explore the world of others. In my experience, your ability to achieve better results in life comes through helping other people to do the same. Whether your needs are emotional, psychological or practical, the chances of them being fulfilled increase when you help others meet their needs.

So how can we achieve this?

In order for this to happen we need to develop a greater understanding and awareness of the people we deal with in our day-to-day lives. We need to get inside the heads of the people we meet in order to see the world from their viewpoint. To explain this further, let me share with you a simple, memorable and powerful illustration.

What is the beachball?

Imagine you are in a large room packed with over a hundred people. In the centre of the room is a large multi-coloured beachball. When I say large, I mean huge. So big in fact, that it stands at

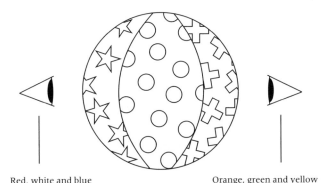

Red, white and blue   Orange, green and yellow

over thirty feet tall and touches the ceiling. Because of its size, the people are squeezed back to the edges of the room. Now here is the interesting part. When you ask people from one side of the room the colour of the beachball they reply, 'Red, white and blue'; yet the people on the opposite side of the room claim to see three different colours; 'orange, green and yellow'. Despite looking at the same beachball, the perspective they are looking from influences the colours they see.

Most people will *not* say, 'Well, from my perspective the beachball is red, white and blue, but I realize it might be different from yours'. No. People tend to believe that what they see is reality. Thanks to the influence of the Greek philosophers Aristotle, Socrates and Plato, our education system in the west has conditioned us to think in logical, either/or, concrete terms. Things are either right or wrong. If from where you are standing the beachball is orange, green and yellow, it cannot also be red, white and blue. To continue the colour theme further, we have a tendency to think in black or white and in right or wrong terms. It seems safe. When we don't, we can be labelled as indecisive. Being open to alternative viewpoints may be seen as a sign of weakness on our part.

People generally are not comfortable with 'grey areas'. It is a place of uncertainty. It is not how we have been taught to see the world. Winning an argument by proving the other person wrong is seen as a virtue. Education is a place where we ask, 'Did you get the answers right?' as opposed to, 'What did you learn?' Such a system of thinking is helpful in some areas such as mathematics, physics or engineering. Whatever side of the beachball you are on, the answer to 3 + 3 is 6. However, when it comes to understanding people and how they see the world, we need to adopt a more flexible way of thinking. You may be familiar with the phrase 'there are always two sides to a story'. Actually there may be more. And each one may be valid. In trying to appreciate how people develop their way of thinking it is helpful to explore what influences how we each see the beachball.

What influences how we and others see the beachball?

There are numerous factors that influence our perspectives. These include our age, values, personality, gender, background, culture, beliefs and many more. For the purpose of this section, let's explore four of them.

Our age influences how we see the beachball

I grew up in the 1960s. When I was young the term 'a big mac' meant a large overcoat you wore when it was raining. My children still look rather bemused when they ask for a 'Big Mac' and I reply, 'Why, is it raining?' The phrase 'going all the way' when I was growing up, meant staying on the bus until it got to the terminus. I understand it has different connotations these days. And I can still remember black and white television, having a choice of only three channels and actually having to physically move off my chair if I wanted to change station. (Boy, we had it tough in those days, but at least we kept fit.)

Age influences our perspective on life. The intro-
duction of new technology into the workplace
may be viewed very differently by someone who
has been using computers since they were a tod-
dler, compared with the individual who never
even used a calculator at school. I am not suggesting people of a certain age group cannot
adapt to technology but for some people, it has
been much more a part of their lives than for
others.

A job for life would have been the expectancy
for many people prior to the 1980s. Now I meet
people in their late 20s who nonchalantly talk
about being made redundant for the second
time in their career. And if you have teenagers
in your household, think of their challenges as
they come to terms with hormonal changes, discovering their sexuality and being caught some-
where between childhood and adulthood.

With age comes experience and invariably, the
older you are, the more experience you have.
How you see and respond to a situation could be
very different from the person who because of
their age has not had an opportunity to acquire
the same amount of experience.

Points to ponder

How does your age influence your views, attitudes and perspectives on life? Think about the ages of those with whom you have close relationships. May this be one reason why you have different perspectives on life?

If you want to win friends and influence people, start by first trying to understand them.

SUMO wisdom

Our values influence how we see the beachball

Let me explain this from a personal perspective.

The personal stuff

My friend Eddie loves his car. It's a Porsche. Not a new one, but one he completely adores and treats almost as though it were his child. Cars do not hold the same appeal for me. I drive a Nissan. It's comfortable, has a few nice gadgets and gets me from A to B. If I find a scratch on my car I am not exactly delighted, but I will soon get over it. Depending on the size of the scratch, on a scale of 1–10 it will probably do well to register a two. Now if that happened to Eddie's car, you would be well advised to keep out of his company and not invade his period of mourning – for about four months. What Eddie and I value is different, and that influences how we see the beachball.

I like gardening. If one of my lupins becomes infested by greenfly, I set about the task of eliminating those vile creatures with military precision. They are the enemy. They must be destroyed. Eddie would not bother.

We can assume that everyone shares the same values as us. The reality is they probably don't. We live and interact with people who may share some of our values but rarely all of them. My work colleague Kate believes if you are not five minutes early for a meeting then you are late. Other people tend to have a more laid back approach to time-keeping, much to Kate's annoyance. One person's reaction to someone being late could be 'so what's the big deal?' Kate may choose to respond a little more assertively.

Our values give us what we believe to be 'the right way' to see the world. It naturally follows in that case, that people who see things differ-

ently from us must have a 'wrong view'. It is this
mindset that thinks 'my way is right and yours
is wrong' that hinders our ability to develop successful relationships. It also explains why people
with similar values may be very different in terms
of personality yet develop successful, long-term
meaningful relationships with each other.

Never assume that other people
value the same things as you.
If you want to develop better
relationships, find out what
is important to the other person.

SUMO
wisdom

Points to ponder

Think of a situation where you don't see eye-to-
eye with another person. Is this due to a clash of
values? Are you prepared to make any compromises? Are they? If not, you may simply have to
accept the limitations of your relationship.

Our personality influences how we see the beachball

Again, let me share with you a personal perspective.

The personal stuff

I have two children. One is loud, outgoing and generally likes to be the centre of attention (she takes after her mother); whilst the other quietly goes about his business, prefers staying in the background and is quite comfortable with silence. Two very different personalities, with neither being right or wrong. These differences however, mean they do not see and respond to situations in the same way. A journey in the car for one of my children is an opportunity to sing and tell stories, whilst for the other it is a chance to be still and reflect on the scenery. Can you relate to any of this?

There are many models for understanding different personality types, the most popular one being devised by Carl Jung, the Swiss psychologist (1875–1961). His aim was to help people understand themselves and others more fully, and explain why people perceive and respond to the world differently. Let me give a simple overview of one way of thinking about the four personality types. Remember, no one fits solely into one type; we would be a blend of all four. However, like a cake recipe, some 'flavours' are more noticeable than others. Let me also stress, this is not intended to be an in-depth look at your personality. I include it purely as some food for thought.

The Cheerleader

An extrovert who gains energy from being around others. They have a tendency to 'wear their emotions on their sleeve'. Cheerleaders thrive on praise and recognition. They can also be impulsive and spontaneous in their opinions and actions, i.e. they often act without thinking and jump quickly to conclusions. Cheerleaders tend not to be the most naturally organized and structured of people, and often attempt a number of tasks at once, starting a new one before finishing the previous one.

Main driver for a cheerleader

Get noticed, get appreciated.

Likely to say

'Well, if you are looking for someone to interview for the company magazine, look no further.'

Unlikely to say

'I've started so I'll finish', or 'Here's a detailed report I prepared earlier'.

How cheerleaders see the beachball

They often see the positive side of the situation and may fail to consider a more cautious perspective. Their viewpoint may fluctuate depending on how they are feeling emotionally.

The Carer

Generally a sociable person who values people contact, although less extrovert than a cheerleader. They prefer to be in the background as opposed to the centre of attention, and are comfortable listening to others as opposed to talking. On less important issues, they will allow others to take the initiative. (Observing two carers deciding where to go for lunch is a fascinating exercise.) They are likely to have a more easy-going approach to life than some people and will do their best to avoid conflict and confrontation. Carers may struggle to say 'no' to people's requests, preferring to say 'yes' rather than run the risk of causing offence. They tend to be more of a follower than a leader.

Main driver for a carer

Get along with others.

Likely to say

'Right, before we start the meeting; how was your weekend?'

Unlikely to say

'OK everyone, I'm in charge here. Now listen up, I have a plan.'

How carers see the beachball

Their perspective is influenced by how the situation affects their relationships. How they feel about an issue can be more important than the facts themselves.

The Commander

An extrovert like the cheerleader, but who is more focused on 'getting things done' with less concern for people. They typically adore 'to-do lists' and love the feeling of achievement when they are able to cross things off their list. Commanders thrive on challenges but their lack of patience comes to the fore when progress is delayed. They tend to be decisive, goal-orientated people who prefer talking to listening. Commanders are likely to make tough demands of themselves and of others, and they enjoy taking charge of a situation.

Main driver for a commander
Get things done.

Likely to say
'Well, that's another two hours wasted. Just exactly how long does it take to give birth these days?'

Unlikely to say
'I would be really interested to hear what other people think.'

How a commander sees the beachball
Could see exploring other people's perspectives as a waste of time, as it delays the need to take action. Focuses on ideas that achieve 'quick wins'.

The Thinker
More of an introvert who gains their energy through reflection and having time to themselves, as opposed to being around people. Like the carer they prefer to listen rather than talk and are more comfortable analyzing data than dealing with people. Thinkers are more likely to take a deliberate, structured analytical approach to a task and are less distracted by feelings and emotions when assessing a situation. They tend

to be cautious in nature and often require copious amounts of detail before making a decision. Thinkers also enjoy giving comprehensive, detailed answers to questions of a technical nature – whether the other person requires it or not. Planning and organizational skills come naturally to a thinker. Being the centre of attention does not.

Main driver for a thinker
   Get this task right.

Likely to say
   'Can you let me think about that and I'll have a detailed report with you inside the next three months.'

Unlikely to say
   'I've just had a crazy idea. How about we organize a staff Christmas pantomime and I can be the lead role.'

How thinkers see the beachball
   May have a tendency to see problems rather than possibilities, and focus on what could go wrong as opposed to why it might work. Could spend so long analyzing the beachball that they fail to make any decision.

OK, review the four personality types. No one is exclusively one type and there will be elements of all four that you can relate to. However, if someone was to push you into a corner and force you to decide which two you identify with most, which would they be? You might not always behave that way but which style are you most comfortable with?

(If you want to complete a quick and easy exercise to help shed some light on your preferred personality style, visit www.TheSumoGuy.com.)

Points to ponder

- What type of personality do you find it most difficult to relate to? Why do you think that is? Think of some positive characteristics of having that type of personality. (The phrase 'I can't think of any' is not acceptable.)
- Think of a relationship that matters to you and consider how your different personality types might help or hinder the way you approach life and tackle problems.

The personal stuff

I guess the personality types I relate to most are the Commander and Cheerleader. My wife Helen is more of a Carer and Thinker. This provides quite a balance when it comes to making decisions, but it can also be a source of frustration for both of us. Whether it is to do with personality or gender I am not sure, but I am always amazed by Helen's behaviour on the telephone. No matter how much of a rush we are in, she insists on asking people how they and their family are before getting to the main purpose of her call. Meanwhile I am thrusting my watch in her face and reminding her that she has already spoken to this person twice today. However, her cautious approach and unwillingness to rush into a decision has saved us money.

Being the spontaneous 'get it done' person that I am, I was quite happy to go along with the first quote we received to have a new kitchen fitted. I liked the guy who came round to measure up and was impressed with his designs. As the quote was within our budget and he could start straight away I was happy to make a decision for the work to commence. My wife insisted that we get three more quotes. To me this was an unnecessary delay and a complete waste of time. We went with the final

> quote. It was better value (i.e. cheaper) and a more innovative design. My 'Thinker wife' had just saved us £500. It was an invaluable lesson for me and a reminder that how I see and respond to an event is not always the best way.

Our current state of mind influences how we see the beachball

Imagine you have just gained promotion at work. You are delighted. You feel good about yourself. Then on the way home you are involved in a minor car accident. The damage is minimal and no one is hurt. You view the incident as a minor inconvenience and nothing more. But what if you hadn't got the promotion? What if you had just been dumped by your partner? How would you respond to the minor accident now? Or if you are stuck in faulty thinking and your Inner Critic is bellowing in your ear, how receptive are you to the 'constructive criticism' your boss wants to give you?

Perhaps you are in 'Hippo Time' and you receive some unwelcome news. How will you respond now? Or maybe you have just got back from the slimming club and won Slimmer of the Week for losing the most weight. When you return home, one of your children asks to borrow the car. What is your likely answer? Would it be the same answer if you had put on weight?

Our view of situations can fluctuate greatly depending on how we are feeling at that particular time. Remember that when you're next communicating to someone, or listening to their story.

Your feelings influence your perceptions.
How are you feeling today?

SUMO wisdom

Points to ponder

If you decide to tackle an issue with someone, consider how they might be currently feeling. And what about your current emotional state? Are you in the best frame of mind to tackle this? Choose your time carefully.

The personal stuff

This next example illustrates the consequences of not seeing someone else's perspective and also why it is necessary to let people know how you see things.

I had bought two tickets to see a football international to be played at Anfield, the home of Liverpool FC. There was only one problem. The game clashed with Helen's birthday and I knew she wasn't a keen fan of football. Having expressed sympathy for such an unfortunate coincidence, I then promptly invited my next-door neighbour to join me at the game. Helen, although disappointed, seemed to appreciate this was a one-off occurrence and took a night in with the children, on her birthday, in her stride. When I was at the match I suddenly had a thought, 'I wonder if Helen would have liked to have been here?' I quickly dismissed such a notion and reasoned with myself, 'If she had wanted to come she would surely have asked'. Meanwhile back at home Helen, I learned later, was thinking the following, 'I wouldn't have minded going to the game tonight. But Paul would have invited me if he wanted me to come'. It was a cracking match. When I returned the kids were in bed and Helen was doing the ironing. Only then did we each share our own perspective on the night's events. Our conversation went something like this.

> **Paul** *'But if I'd known you wanted to come, of course I would have invited you.'*
> **Helen** *'Then why didn't you ask me?'*

> **Paul** *'Well, you don't like football.'*
>
> **Helen** *'So?'*
>
> **Paul** *'Well, I thought you would have said something if you were that keen to go.'*
>
> **Helen** *'I shouldn't have to. You should know.'*
>
> **Paul** *'Know what exactly?'*
>
> **Helen** *'That it would have been nice to be asked.'*
>
> **Paul** *'Look, I'm really sorry. Can we have an early night and forget all about it?'*
>
> **Helen** *'No.'*

We both assumed that the other person understood our view of the beachball. I believed if Helen wanted to go to the game she would have asked me, and Helen believed if I wanted her to go, I would have invited her. We now recognize that not only do we need to take time out to see the other person's perspective, we also need to take responsibility to communicate how we are seeing things.

How to recognize when you're only seeing your side of the beachball

It is easy to spot when this is occurring. Simply notice the language you start to use. Make a mental note of any of the following you have found yourself saying.

- 'Why can't you see it my way?' (Have you tried to see it 'their way'?)

- 'I don't understand my kids. They never listen to a word I say.' (How can you understand someone when you are doing all the talking?)

- 'Why can't you be reasonable?' (Presumably you have decided what 'reasonable' means, i.e. to see and respond to the world the way you do.)

- 'What planet are you on?' (Well, maybe it is time to enter their space and find out.)

- 'That music is awful. You've no taste.' (In truth we all have taste, it's just that not everyone shares yours.)

- 'They can be so boring.' (You mean, they don't meet your criteria of what interesting and exciting is like.)

- 'There is only one way to handle this problem.' (In fact, there could be a number of alternatives, but you are going with the first one that comes to mind.)

Get the picture? Actually, we probably don't get the full picture unless we are prepared to remove our blinkers. Most of us (including myself) need reminding of how many different ways the world can be viewed and the factors that influence people's perspective. But does appreciating others' viewpoints mean I have to agree with it?

Understanding does not mean agreeing

Discovering someone's perspective, and understanding the reasons for their views, does not necessarily mean we agree and embrace them ourselves. You will meet some very sincere people who hold very strong opinions on life. You may believe them to be sincerely wrong. However, if you want to persuade them at least to consider another viewpoint, but begin with the attitude, 'I am right, you are wrong', it will do little to encourage meaningful dialogue. When you begin with the attitude, 'Let me first try to understand why you think and behave the way you do', you're more likely to encourage an open and honest discussion. When you feel people have listened to you and tried to understand you, then you are more likely to listen to them.

SUMO
wisdom

People are less defensive when you seek to understand their viewpoint rather than try to dismantle it.

Having looked at *why* people see the beachball differently, let's look at *how* we go about understanding another person's viewpoint.

How to move forward

If you have not done so already, identify a relationship that you know needs to improve. Perhaps you have failed to see the other person's side of the beachball up until now, or you have failed to communicate how things look from your perspective. A willingness to *Shut Up* the old approach and *Move On* to a different strategy may now be required. Here are some practical ideas on how to help the process. The relevance of some of the ideas will depend on the context of the conversation.

- Firstly, do not attempt to have a conversation when both of you are angry. You will both be in primitive brain and 'discussion' is likely to become an argument. At least one of you needs to be in 'rational brain'.

- Work hard at actively listening and indicate to the other person through your body language that you are. Make some eye contact, avoid distractions (such as the computer or the television being on) and give this person your full attention. Their perception of whether or not you are listening is crucial.

- Don't interrupt the other person and take over the conversation. Allow them to vent.

- Don't finish off the other person's sentences. This can give the impression you are rushing them and sometimes you get it wrong.

- Work hard at trying to understand their perspective. Put aside preconceived ideas of what you think their view is.

- As you listen, look for what you can agree with, rather than focus on what divides you.

- When they have finished speaking, the first question to ask is, 'Is there anything else you would like to add?' This prevents you from jumping in immediately with your perspective. It also provides the other person with an opportunity to summarize their points, and perhaps re-emphasize an issue that is important to them.

• Before moving on to share your perspective, ask questions to gain clarification, e.g. 'When you said … can you explain that a little more?' or 'Can you give me an example of that, please?' This is not done to make the other person defensive, but in order genuinely to understand their view.

• It is now your turn to share how you see things. Ensure the behaviour you have modelled is followed by the other person. (This might require you having to be assertive if they start to interrupt you or do not allow you to finish.)

Helpful phrases to use

The following phrases may prove helpful in your conversation. However, use language and terminology you are comfortable with. These are just some examples:

'Help me understand your perspective on this.'

'Can we explore some options on how best to deal with this situation?'

'I would be really interested to know what you think.'

'I'm conscious I'm only seeing things from my perspective; what would your view be?'

'Maybe I've been a bit inflexible in my approach up until now.'

(And when you need to communicate your perspective ...)

'Can I shed some light on how I see things?'

'Let me fill you in on how things look from my perspective.'

'I'd value you giving me some time to share my take on things.'

'I appreciate you might not be aware of all the facts from my viewpoint, so let me elaborate.'

These ideas and phrases are intended to help the process. They will not guarantee a successful outcome, but they do increase the chances.

Points to ponder

Sometimes it is completely acceptable and appropriate to stand your ground. But not always. How are your stubbornness and unwillingness to be flexible helping the situation? How is insisting that you are right helping to move things forward? Which phrases might you consider using? Is the other person aware of your perspective?

The personal stuff

Angela, a friend of mine, has not spoken to her mother for two years.

The reason for this silence is all to do with her mother – or so Angela believes. Angela believes she is in the right and her mother is in the wrong; therefore, why should she have to make the first move towards some kind of reconciliation with her mum? Angela has two small children. They do not know their grandma.

Move things forward by challenging the golden rule

You may have come across a concept called 'the golden rule'. Many people believe it to be the best advice you can have on how to build successful relationships. Personally I'm not so sure. Here's why:

The golden rule states the following: 'Treat people as you would want to be treated'. This seems a fairly noble view, and it's true regarding the ethics and morality of our behaviour. However, in terms of communication style and personality preferences, it's not always helpful. Does an introverted, middle-aged 'Thinker' who has recently got married and moved to the countryside want to be treated in the same way as a young, recently divorced 'Cheerleader' who has just started work in the city?

The SUMO rule is this:

> 'Not everyone wants to be treated in the same way as you do.
> Treat people as they want to be treated.'

Most people do want to be dealt with fairly, honestly and with respect. But after that, it is up to us to find out what works best for them. When you do, you are better equipped to achieve a more favourable outcome. So challenge conventional wisdom and be prepared to bring a new perspective to things.

The joy of a new perspective

Life can become quite interesting when you look at things from a new angle. I came across this piece recently. I hope you enjoy it. It is titled: 'The George Carlin Theory'.*

> *The most unfair thing about life is the way it ends …*
> *I mean, life is tough. It takes up a lot of your time and what do you get at the end of it? Death. I mean, what's that, a bonus? I think the life cycle is all backwards. You should die first, get it out of the way. Then you move to an old people's home. You get kicked out when you're too young, you get a gold watch and then you go to work. You work for forty years until you're young enough to enjoy your retirement. You have fun, party plenty, then you get ready for senior school. Then you go to junior school, you become a kid, you play and you have no responsibilities. You become a little baby, you go back into the womb, spend your last nine months floating … and you finish off as an orgasm.*

*The American comedian George Carlin did not write this piece and the actual author remains unknown.

In a nutshell

The ability to succeed in life is inextricably linked to our ability to deal with people. To know how best to deal with others we need to start with trying to understand them. When we appreciate how and why people view the world differently and respond appropriately to that, we are able to connect and engage with them at a completely new level.

SUMO summary

- A brilliant life comes through better relationships.
- In order to meet your needs, help others to achieve theirs.
- Two opposing views does not necessarily mean one has to be wrong.
- Remember the beachball. *Shut Up* believing your perspective is the only one and *Move On* to seeing how the world looks through someone else's eyes.
- Four factors that influence how we see things are:
  - Our age
  - Our values
  - Our personality
  - Our current state of mind.

- Understanding someone's viewpoint does not necessarily mean you agree with it.
- When people feel you are trying to understand them, they are more likely to try and understand you.
- *Shut Up* waiting for the other person to take the initiative. Move On to being a peacemaker.

Chapter 5

Learn Latin

We have now explored four SUMO principles. But here is the harsh reality. Despite the insights and ideas you have gained so far, they may result in little or no change in your life. This fifth principle will explore why we can be full of good intentions and yet fail to make those intentions reality. You will discover the reasons why we procrastinate and how to overcome it. Or to put it another way; how you can *Shut Up* the excuses and *Move On* to action.

Let me begin by sharing a personal experience of my struggle to take action.

The personal stuff

In the spring of 1991 I set up my own business, working as a freelance trainer and speaker. Times were tough. The economic boom of the 80s was over and Britain was officially in recession. My 'office' doubled as a bedroom, so I had a desk, a telephone and a double bed. It was a challenge (particularly for Bob and Linda in the double bed). As I sat at my desk, I faced a list of names and telephone numbers of people who I needed to contact. Deep down ... actually, not even deep down, I dreaded having to make a single call. I began to fantasize (not all fantasies are positive you know) about the reactions I would receive. 'They're tied up at the moment'; 'Can you call back ... in four years'; or just a simple, 'No thank you'.

I hated cold calling and quite quickly became enveloped by the 'phantom of procrastination'. As it was 1.30 p.m., I convinced myself that most people would still be on lunch and to wait another half-hour. Two o'clock arrived and I then persuaded myself that I was overcome with an incredible urge for coffee. Making my way downstairs to the kitchen, I became distracted by plants that needed watering and plates that needed washing. Thirty minutes passed. It was 2.30 p.m. and all excuses had dried up (or so I thought). It was actually time to make those cold calls.

But then came a flash of inspiration. A conversation unfolded within my mind. How many people are still at work at 2.30 p.m. on a Friday afternoon? Even those that are, are not likely to want to discuss their training requirements. Their thoughts will already be focused on the weekend. I will leave those calls to Monday, I reasoned to myself. Phew, what a relief; the difficult and uncomfortable task of cold calling had been put off for a few days.

I had convinced myself that there was no point in taking any immediate action and in doing so, had missed out on the opportunity of winning more business. However, I had achieved my goal – to avoid rejection and not do anything uncomfortable. Sound familiar?

Procrastination came easily to me, but then I saw the film *Dead Poets Society*. It was to provide the perfect antidote. At one stage in the film, Robin Williams, who plays the lead role of an English teacher at an American all boys public school, teaches his pupils a Latin phrase. In an attempt to inspire these young men not to take their lives for granted, he teaches them the phrase *carpe diem*. Loosely translated, this means 'seize the day'. I was inspired by the film and made a poster with the phrase 'Carpe Diem, Seize the Day' written on it, which I hung on my office wall. (Bob and Linda were cool about it.)

The next day I was watching the BBC Television comedy *Only Fools and Horses*. Two brothers run a market stall in south-east London; however, times are tough and money is short. In an attempt to motivate his younger brother Rodney, Delboy utters a version of the SAS motto 'Who Dares Wins'. Delboy's exact words were 'He who dares, wins'.

I liked the phrase. It was what I needed to hear. I made my second makeshift poster for my office wall and when I heard the 'phantom of procrastination' whisper in my ear, I now felt I at least had two phrases to inspire me into taking action.

Points to ponder

What are some of the things you try to put off doing? Do you procrastinate more at home or at work? How often does it happen?

So why do we procrastinate?

Let's explore five reasons why people 'put things off' and fail to *carpe diem* and take action in their lives. (These reasons have been inspired by my friends at The Mind Gym, www.themindgym.com.)

Reason 1 — avoiding discomfort

Achieving success means that at times, we have to leave our 'comfort zone'. We may have to move out of our world of familiarity, safety and security and do things that we would not normally do. When we do something new or different, it can feel strange. This can result in a negative response initially because many people subconsciously, live by the mantra:

'If it feels good, do it.'

Likewise, they can also live by the reverse of this mantra:

'If it doesn't feel good – don't do it.'

Although there are exceptions, our tendency as human beings is to take the path of least resistance. We look for the magic pill, the magic patch, the magic exercise machine. Products that promise 'successful outcomes' with little or no long-term effort on our part will always be popular.

Successful people think differently. They understand that if they are to achieve a positive result in any area of life, then they have to be prepared to face their 'discomfort' head on. Whether it is getting fit or going for a new job, life will present us with challenges. If we are to succeed, this will involve us taking action or thinking in a way that moves us beyond our normal zone of comfort and familiarity.

Blessed are the people who do the
uncomfortable,
for they will often be successful.

SUMO
wisdom

Points to ponder

What are some of the things you feel uncomfortable having to do? What is the cause of your discomfort?

Reason 2 — emotional barriers

Whether we decide to take action or not can be
dependent on how we feel. For example, I am
going to write that report, tidy the garage, or go
on that diet, *when I feel motivated*. Or I am waiting
to *feel creative* before I tackle that problem. Put
simply, emotions can take our actions hostage.

When you remain a prisoner
to your emotions, you may never
know the freedom of success.

SUMO
wisdom

Reason 3 — fear of failure

It is easy to develop the following mindset: 'if I don't attempt something, then I can never be accused of failing'. That is true. Equally, however, if I never attempt anything, I will never experience the feelings of achievement and success. Some people are quite happy to stand on the sidelines and point out where others go wrong, yet they themselves lack the courage to dare to fail.

SUMO wisdom

If you want to achieve anything in life, remember, setbacks come with the territory.

From our childhood, we can become conditioned to believe that if we attempt something and fail, that this is in some way wrong. Education has, in some cases, encouraged us to find '*the* right answer' rather than to experiment and discover many right answers. (We explored some of this in Chapter 4.) Behind some people's behaviour is the underlying belief that, 'I must be right, I must be perfect'. Attempting something that may expose weaknesses or lack of knowledge will be avoided by some people. Fear of failure, or perhaps more importantly, the fear of *being seen by others to have failed*, will trap some people into never taking action.

Failure isn't fatal until you stop trying.

SUMO wisdom

Points to ponder

What has the fear of failure prevented you from doing?

Reason 4 — complacency

'There's no rush', 'I'll wait till the kids have left home', 'I'll quit smoking in the New Year'. There always seems to be some reason why we can put off taking action today. What can drive this attitude is a false belief that there is plenty of time to accomplish all we want to achieve. But when tomorrow does come, we find another excuse to avoid taking action.

Complacency can also occur due to the mistaken belief that life is something that happens to you as opposed to something you can influence. (We will look at this in more detail in our final SUMO principle.) A lack of goals and sense of purpose in our lives, results in people drifting along in a haze of complacency.

SUMO wisdom

Wake up and smell the coffee.
Life at its longest is still fairly short.
Shut Up the voice of complacency
and Move On to what's important.

Points to ponder

In what areas of your life have you allowed complacency to creep in? Your career? Relationships? Home improvements? Finance? Fitness? All of them?

Reason 5 — action illusion

Some people can always appear busy. The question is, busy doing what? Rather than admit that they don't want to do a task, they use a lack of time as their excuse. People can talk about what they are going to do, hold meetings to discuss how they are going to do it and even draw up plans outlining what they will do. This may all be very useful initially, but there comes a time when we need to start taking action.

When all is said and done,
more is said than done.

**SUMO
wisdom**

We saw from our first SUMO principle that on a day-to-day basis, we do so much on auto-pilot, i.e. without thinking. Maybe we need to ask ourselves, 'Am I confusing activity with effectiveness?'

> **Points to ponder**
>
> Are your activities and your busyness hiding the fact that you do not want to address the really important issues in your life right now?

So we have explored why people procrastinate; now we need to examine how to overcome it.

Where do we go from here?

Some people may be tempted to say the following: 'Okay, big deal. I procrastinate. Doesn't everyone?' Well actually – no! Some people have decided to take responsibility and to take action. Now, there is no 'Procrastinators Anonymous' support group (although there have been a number of people who have thought about setting one up, but never got round to it). So how are we going to tackle this unhelpful, debilitating habit that can rob us of achieving success and happiness in life? Here are some strategies that people use to defeat procrastination.

How to conquer the procrastination habit

Just start it

That's right, just do something. Do not worry about completing the task or how much time it will take to finish – just start it. Yes, I know you are not in the mood and you are not feeling motivated. Tough. SUMO!

Right feelings follow right actions.
Shut Up the dithering,
Move On to the acting.

SUMO
wisdom

The personal stuff

For two years I had contemplated tidying my garage. Two years! Then one day, when I had a spare
half-hour before lunch, I decided to make a start.
(Even though I knew it would probably take at least
half a day.) Within five minutes, I found a level of
enthusiasm rising up within me I had not known
before. I discovered things I never realized we even
had ... an old motorbike, a garden gnome, two
children. (Alright, the garden gnome is perhaps
an exaggeration.)

Picture what success looks like and how it feels
Think about the task you know you need to
tackle. Perhaps it is quitting smoking, losing
weight, speaking in public, or flying for the first
time. Now I want you to close your eyes and imagine what success will look and feel like. What
do you see? What are you able to do now, that
you were unable to do before? How does it feel
to have conquered that fear of flying or speak-

ing? When you've quit smoking, how will you feel about yourself? Whatever your challenge, imagine the outcome you want rather than the activities required to get you there. Focusing on your destination rather than the journey can inspire you to take action.

Now imagine your life in five years' time if you decided to do nothing. What does your world look like now? What are the consequences of you not taking action? Visualize it. How does that make you feel? Is that what you want for your future?

Do the nasties first

Each day people are faced with tasks they would prefer not to do. It could be a telephone call to make or a person to meet. All of us can be tempted to tackle the more pleasurable tasks first and then leave the nasties until later. Guess what? Sometimes we find that we've not had enough time to tackle our nasties. What a pity. Never mind, you'll get round to it tomorrow. Then when you wake up the next day, what have you got to look forward to? Tackling the 'nasties'. So, what does that do to your levels of motivation?

Eat your sprouts first.
Then you can enjoy
the rest of your meal.
Shut Up on the niceties,
Move On to the nasties.

SUMO wisdom

Not all 'nasties' are as bad as we would expect. But some are – that's why they are called 'nasties'. I am not asking you to convince yourself that 'nasties' are really nice. I am saying tackle them first – unless you can prove in a court of law that the more pleasurable task you embarked upon is in fact more important.

Reward your progress

Once you decide to take action, reward your progress. Just finished a nasty? Good, so what is your mini reward? (I suggest a mini reward or else this conquering procrastination routine could get rather expensive.) It might be to go and see a film, have a coffee break, or simply decide to ring that friend you wanted a chat with. I am going to reward myself with a teacake after I have finished writing this chapter. (Oh, the life of an international speaker and author.) Remember, if it's a task that will take a long time to complete, then we need to set ourselves some milestones and reward our progress. Rewarding yourself only after you have finished the task may not be motivating enough. A friend of mine who wanted to lose weight bought a CD for every 7lb shed. Another friend filled a jar with all the money saved from quitting smoking and spent it on a family holiday.

> **SUMO wisdom**
>
> *Focus on progress not perfection and reward yourself accordingly.*

Make a date with a mate

The sad fact of life is that only a small percentage of people reading this book will take any action as a result. But what if you knew that you were attending a workshop in four weeks' time and had to report to the group on what actions you had taken as a result of reading this book? The chances are, the percentage of people who would take action would increase significantly. (Hence I often run follow-up sessions to my workshops.)

A 'mate' does not need to be a friend, but someone who you are happy to share your issue with and who is committed to following up on your progress. They must also have your permission to challenge you if you're not taking the action you said you would.

> **The personal stuff**
>
> My work as a life coach brings positive results in people's lives, partly because they have someone to support them and someone they feel accountable to. Ultimately, my clients are only accountable to themselves, but the discipline of having to feedback their progress results in more focused actions being taken by them.

Shut Up trying to do it on your own,
Move On to finding a mate
to support you.

SUMO
wisdom

Challenge your complacency
Perhaps the most powerful way I can challenge your complacency is to ask you to consider the following.

Imagine seven people lined up in a row:

Now imagine each person represents a day of the week.

Mon   Tue   Wed   Thu   Fri   Sat   Sun

Now imagine each day of the week represents a decade of your life.

0–10y 11–20y 21–30y 31–40y 41–50y 51–60y 61–70y

So which day of the week are you on? I am on Thursday night, soon to move into Friday. For me the weekend is fast approaching and for some of you it has already arrived.

Now, before all those who are reading this get too depressed because you are already at the week-end, consider this. If you are living a healthy lifestyle, you can add another two people to your line-up (making a total of nine people), as there is a good chance you will get a Bank Holiday Monday and Tuesday as well.

Remember, it's never too late to take action. I am inspired by people such as Winston Churchill. He became Prime Minister for a second time on the Bank Holiday Monday of his life. So whatever day of the week you are on, perhaps it is time to take the necessary action to make sure the journey is not just a good one, but a great one. You owe it to yourself and those around you to challenge your complacency. (Our next SUMO principle will help you to make the rest of your 'week' a significant and successful one.)

> Zig Ziglar said, 'At the end of your days do not be the kind of person who says I wish I had, I wish I had, I wish I had. Be the kind of person who says I'm glad I did, I'm glad I did, I'm glad I did.'

SUMO wisdom

Those are some ideas on how to conquer our procrastination habit. Now it's time to use them. Work through the following questions, preferably with a 'mate'. Only when you have finished the exercise can you have a mini reward.

SUMO exercise

1   Choose a task or issue that you need to take action on.

2   Why is this important to you?

3   What are the consequences if you take no action?

4   Picture and feel what success will look like when you've achieved your objective.

5   Which 'procrastinators' hinder your progress? (i.e. avoiding discomfort, emotional barriers, fear of failure, action illusion and complacency.)

6   What actions will you take to tackle this issue?

7   When will you start?

8   How will you reward your progress?

9   Who will be your 'mate'?

You can e-mail me with your progress and successes at:sumo@paulmcgee.com

The personal stuff

So how has learning and living by the Latin phrase *carpe diem* helped me? The turning point in my business came in 1994. I had just received an information pack from an organization that ran business seminars in America, Europe and Asia. They were now looking for British-based speakers to develop their work further in the UK. They particularly wanted to hear from trainers or speakers who were comfortable addressing large audiences (I mean in terms of numbers, not weight) and who enjoyed 'performing' and delivering their material in an entertaining way. With all due modesty, I have to admit I thought the job specification had been written specifically with me in mind. (My next book will be on the subject of developing personal humility.)

Then I came to the section marked 'method of application'. It said the following: 'Please apply by sending in a one-hour video of yourself, speaking ideally in front of 50 to 100 people.' It then added, 'If you do not possess such a video, you are probably not ready to join us yet'. The excitement that had been welling up inside of me immediately drained away. At that point in my career, I spoke mainly to groups of around a dozen people, and I quickly realized that my two main clients were un-likely to allow their training sessions to be filmed. My hopes of international travel and speaking in front of large audiences had been crushed with the reading of one sentence.

Realizing there was no possible way I could meet their application criteria, I reluctantly placed the information pack in the bin. Then I looked up. On the wall in front of me, were two makeshift posters with the phrases 'Carpe Diem, Seize the Day' and 'Who Dares Wins'. I couldn't ignore them. They seemed to compel me to reach back into the bin and pull out the discarded information pack. The wording under the 'method of application' section had not changed – but the mindset of the person reading it had.

As I read the form now, I was determined that I would apply for the position. Rather than accept the reality of the situation, I was now beginning to think of possible solutions around it. The form still stated, *'please apply by sending a one-hour video of yourself, speaking ideally in front of 50 to 100 people'*. However my eyes immediately focused on the word, *'ideally'*. 'Paul, we don't live in an ideal world,' I thought to myself, and a plan began to unfold in my mind. Hire a room, invite a few friends and get my wife, Helen, to film a one-hour session of me delivering my best material.

Yet almost immediately a barrage of 'what ifs' flooded into my mind. What if you cannot find a room to hire? What if your friends cannot make it? What if you fail? Reasons to procrastinate began to line up in my head. I realized that taking action would require me to move out of my comfort zone. There was also the possibility that I might have to explain my failure to a number of people if the organization rejected my application. But how would I feel if I did not apply? Would such an opportunity come along again, and if so, when? I then allowed myself to dwell on another 'what if' question. 'What if I succeed?'

My *carpe diem* mindset was now very much in charge and I began to put my plan into action. Hiring a room was straightforward, but what about renting a crowd? I rang all my friends and put forward my proposition. 'There will be free food, free drink, just laugh in the right places'. Having rung all my friends and convinced both to attend (you remember Bob and Linda, don't you?), I then realized that although 50 people was unrealistic, an audience of two was perhaps a little on the low side.

Eventually with the support of some family and a few people who would subject themselves to anything at the thought of free food (I knew a couple of students), my audience swelled to a grand total of eight. After filming, I submitted my video (some, but not all, of my audience laughed in the right places), making it clear to the organization that what they were watching was a contrived scenario.

But what did I have to lose? Well, my Inner Critic kept reminding me that actually, I could 'look really stupid', but I chose to recall the phrase 'Who Dares Wins'. Several weeks later I finally received a telephone call. The organization had watched my video and wanted to meet me. Eventually they hired me. They became my largest client and working for them was a turning point, not just in my business, but in my life also. Within three years of sending the video filmed in front of eight people in Warrington, I was presenting seminars to hundreds of people in places like Hong Kong, Malaysia and Singapore. On this occasion I had conquered my procrastination habit and was now reaping the rewards. But I still look back on my life before this time and wish I had learnt the lesson sooner. How much longer will you wait?

Don't leave your dreams in the bin.
Shut Up the voice that says 'no way',
Move On to the voice that says
'Why not?'

SUMO wisdom

Points to ponder

It will have been easy to read through this chapter and ignore the exercises, and not really take time to consider the questions raised. If that's what you've done I guarantee that reading this book will not help you creat a brilliant life. But if you do take action, well who knows what you might achieve? Our final SUMO principle will provide some answers to that question.

In a nutshell

Great ideas, great goals and great intentions are meaningless without great actions. People achieve success in life not just because they take charge of their thinking, but because their thinking propels them into taking action.

SUMO summary

- Life rewards intelligent action, not intention.
- People fail to take action for a variety of reasons. Avoiding discomfort, emotional barriers, fear of failure, complacency and action illusion.
- Procrastination is a debilitating habit that can rob you of success and happiness.
- Tactics to conquer the procrastination habit include;

  Just start it. Shut Up the dithering, Move On to the acting

  What does success look and feel like?

  Do the nasties first. Shut Up on the niceties, Move On to the nasties.

  Reward your progress.

  Make a date with a mate. Shut Up trying to do it on your own, Move On to finding a mate to support you.

  Challenge your complacency. Shut Up the voice of complacency, Move On to what is important.

- Shut Up believing reading this book is enough; Move On to doing something.

Chapter 6

Ditch Doris Day

O K, I confess, this may seem a strange title for our sixth SUMO principle. So let me explain.

Why Doris Day?

In 1956, Jay Livingston and Ray Evans wrote the song 'Que Sera Sera' for the Alfred Hitchcock movie *The Man Who Knew Too Much*. It was sung by Doris Day. One of the lines is as follows:

> *'Que sera, sera,*
> *Whatever will be, will be,*
> *The future's not ours to see ...'*

Doris Day, who at the time of writing is in her 80s, is still esteemed as a wonderful actress and singer and is adored by fans around the world. Doris, this is not personal. But our final SUMO principle is this: if we want to experience a brilliant life we must rid ourselves of the *laissez faire* attitude, 'Whatever will be, will be'. Let's be honest. How inspiring is that? I recognize unexpected events will occur in your life and mine, but I belicve we can still plan and work towards a future *we* want to see. This is what our final success principle is all about; creating our future.

Firstly, let's remind ourselves of the five previous SUMO success principles.

Our five SUMO principles so far are:

1   Take responsibility for your life (*Change Your T-shirt*).

2   Take charge of your thinking *(Develop Fruity Thinking)*.

3   Understand how setbacks affect you and how to recover from them. *(Hippo Time Is OK)*.

4   Increase your understanding and awareness of other people's world *(Remember The Beach-ball)*

5   Change comes through action not intention *(Learn Latin)*.

Now your aim is to take those five principles and apply them in helping you to 'create and enjoy a brilliant life'. But first you need to decide what kind of future you want.

> **SUMO wisdom**

Your destiny has not been decided. Neither the moon, the stars nor fate determine it — you do.

What kind of future do you want?

Several years ago, I heard the American sociologist and church leader Dr Anthony Campolo address a large gathering of sales people. He recalled some research he had come across in which a group of elderly people, all of whom were aged 95 or over, were asked the following question: 'If you were to live your life over again, what would you do differently next time?' Now that is an interesting question. And it is one I would like you to think about. Why wait until you're too old to do anything about it before considering such an important issue?

Now you are probably wondering what these elderly people answered. (If you're not, you should be. Where is your sense of curiosity?) According to Campolo, the three top answers were summarized as follows:

Have less regrets

It seems this was related more to what people didn't do as opposed to what they did do in their lives.

Take time out to reflect more
Some people felt they just drifted along with the crowd and spent little if any time considering what *they* really wanted from life.

Leave a legacy
People wanted to feel that their life on earth had counted for something and that in some way their life would be remembered after they had gone.

Now, how old are you? I want you to imagine what might be a scary scenario. Tomorrow will be your last day on this planet and you are asked the same question: 'If you were to live your life over again, what would you do differently next time?' What would your top three answers be? (You can write them below if you like.)

My top three answers would be:

1

2

3

I find it interesting that most people will write a will about what they want to happen to their affairs after they die. It requires some time and effort to sort out a will. However, fewer people seem to put the same effort and attention into what they want to happen whilst they are alive. Although they might not consciously think it, some people's behaviour indicates they are living by the philosophy 'Whatever will be, will be'. How about you?

Food for thought? I hope so. Now your answers to the following questions will determine whether you 'Ditched Doris Day' long ago or whether you are still embracing a 'Que Sera, Sera' view of life.

1　Have you ever considered what success means to you? Yes/No

2　Do you have some specific, clearly defined goals that you wish to achieve in life? (The goal 'being happy' is not a specific goal.) Yes/No

3　If you have some goals, have you shared them with someone close to you? Yes/No

4　Do you have some plans in place to help you achieve your goals? Yes/No

5   Have you thought about the kind of memo-
     ries you would like your family and friends
     to have of you? Yes/No

If you have more no's than yes's you have a decision to make. Either do something about it or
don't. The choice is yours. This is your life. My
goal is not to shame you or make you feel guilty.
It is simply to share some insights, raise some
questions and make you aware of some possibilities. If you are happy with your life as it is now,
fine. Congratulations. I guess you are living the
life you always wanted. Or have you simply ad-
justed your expectations, limited your dreams
and decided to settle for what you have?

Do not adjust your goals to bring them in line with your life. Adjust your life to bring you in line with your goals.

SUMO wisdom

If you had more yes's than no's – congratulations.
However, whatever your answers, the next few
pages will either confirm the kind of future you
want or help you to create it.

Points to ponder

How will you ensure you have no regrets? How often do you take time out to consider what you really want from life? What will your legacy be?

Let's go back to the five questions I asked above. Your answers are the starting point to creating your desired future. And if your future focus seems a little fuzzy at the moment, don't worry. As Zig Ziglar said, 'Go as far as you can and when you get there you'll see further.'

Here again is the first question.

What does success mean to you?

It is important to come up with your own definition of success rather than focus on what you think other people see it as. People can be caught in the trap of living their life to please others rather than the life they choose. In such cases success is hollow and ultimately unfulfilling.

To help you focus on what success means to you, I would encourage you to read the next piece of 'The personal stuff' and then the lessons that follow.

The personal stuff

I used to have a warped and unbalanced view of success. I had never consciously considered what success meant to me, but on reflection, two areas were important: how much I earned and how much I weighed. Mistakenly I believed that if I achieved a certain level of income and was a particular weight, then I would be successful. And achieving success, I assumed, would equate to being happy. I was wrong. Very wrong. On 24 December 1997 my wife and I embarked upon our usual Christmas Eve ritual. After our children went to bed (they were aged four and two at the time) we would share a meal together and exchange a couple of presents. It was an opportunity to reflect back on the year, to talk about our highs and lows and share our hopes for the coming year. But this time was different. I was in a relatively upbeat mood. This had been a good year. I had achieved my financial goals, completed another book and was within a couple of pounds of my ideal weight. Not only that, but I had spoken in Hong Kong, Malaysia and Singapore and visited (on my own) a family friend in Australia.

Helen's view of the year was very different. It had been a year when she and the children had seen very little of me. When I was at home my whole focus was work-related and I had become increasingly irritable with her and the children. All that seemed to matter to me was what was going on in my world. Was I successful in business? Yes. Was I being a good husband and father? No. If things continued unchanged for the next couple of years would we remain married? Unlikely. I had been blind to my behaviour and the impact my attitude was having on my family. Finally Helen explained what things looked like from her side of the beach-ball. It was the wake-up call I needed. It was time to broaden my definition of success.

Broadening your definition of success

As a result of this experience I identified four key aspects of my life that I needed to keep a check on. Although I list them separately, they are not independent of each other. They all interrelate in some way and are all equally important. The first one is optional depending on your circumstances. If this is the case, you may want to view it as 'work', which may be paid or unpaid.

1 Career. I also include finance in this area. My business is still very important to me and I do still spend time away from home. But my view of work has changed. It is no longer the sole definition of who I am as a person. I have learnt to take myself a little less seriously, to delegate more and to learn the art of saying 'no' when appropriate. Previously my family's needs came further down my list of priorities than my clients. I would never admit to this of course, but my behaviour revealed the truth. I didn't even realize it. My clients and cash flow are still important, but so too are my family. My desire for work–life fulfilment (which I believe is a more helpful term than work–life balance) came about through a change in my attitude. I need to focus on my career but not to the detriment of the rest of my life

2   *Relationships.* I had taken my family for granted and when I was at home, my mind was still on work. I now appreciate how fortunate I am. Now I do not just plan my work, I plan family activities. This does not simply include holidays or a weekend away, but what I term 'family nights'. No phone calls are answered, no friends can come after school. This is simply our time together. We enjoy a favourite meal and either a DVD or a few games. My relationship with friends is also important. They help me see things in perspective and are very good at helping me keep my feet firmly on the ground. Fun time with friends is crucial for me. Remember, the quality of your

relationships underpins all you do. (A group called the Relationship Foundation have coined the term 'Relationship Pension'. The idea is that if we are to have a fulfilled life in the future, we not only need to invest our finances, but also invest in our relationships. They can be contacted at www.relationshipsfoundation.org.)

3   *Recreation.* I include health and leisure time in this dimension of my life. Health for me incorporates my physical, psychological and spiritual well-being. My faith is fundamental to who I am as a person, and I value time to reflect, to pray and to enjoy moments of silence. When I exercise either by going for long walks or visits to the gym, it helps my physical and mental well-being. My times of recreation literally provide opportunities to 're-create'. To thrive in a demanding, fast-paced world, we all need times of recovery and moments to relax. Strangely, watching Bradford City meets some of these needs as well as providing time to be with my son and my friends. (What it does for my psychological well-being is open to discussion, however.)

4   *Contribution.* My life had become so self-absorbed I rarely considered the needs of others. I

have since discovered the strangest secret. It really can be better to give than to receive. That is what contribution is about. I feel more fulfilled now that I view my time, talent and money not just as an opportunity to meet my needs, but also those of others. It is quite liberating when you become less inward looking. Making a contribution to others, in whatever way, makes you feel better about yourself.

Reviewing these four equally important dimensions of who I am and what I do is a good 'life check'. It is a process I go through regularly, usually on a monthly basis. Christmas Eve with Helen has been better since I did this (as well as the rest of the times I see her) and I'm also managing my stress levels much more effectively. Business is still good and I now feel much closer to my children. It's not a perfect life, but it's better than before. (It's just a pity about the football team I support.)

Even when your car is running well, it's still good to have it serviced. The same goes for your life. When did you last have a check-up?

SUMO wisdom

So what about you? Consider what success means to you, in relation to the following:

- *Career* (or your paid or unpaid work) – Success means …

- *Relationships* – Success means …

- *Recreation* – Success means …

- *Contribution* – Success means …

Now, let's go on to look at the second question …

Do you have some clearly defined goals that you wish to achieve in life?

It is good to have goals. They provide focus, direction, motivation, purpose and feedback. They can be in any area of our lives. Trust me, when times are tough – the traffic is bad, the builders are late and the boss is being difficult – your ability to cope will improve if there is something you are aiming for that is bigger than all those challenges. Review the Career, Relationships,

Recreation and Contribution aspects of your life. Set yourself a goal in each area. Let's start with the short term. What would you like to achieve in the next 12 months? Write down your goals below.

1   My Career (or work) goal over the next 12 months is …

2   My Relationship goal over the next 12 months is …

3   My Recreation goal over the next 12 months is …

4   My Contribution goal over the next 12 months is …

Now let's think long term. Dream a little if you like and come up with the top ten things you want to do before you leave this planet.

Top ten things to do before I leave this planet

1

2

3

4

5

6

7

8

9

10

Vicky, a delegate on one of my workshops, did a similar exercise. She decided on the ten things she wanted to do during the next year. Included in her top ten were: wanting to spend a night at the Ritz Hotel in London; to ride a horse; have her hair styled at Vidal Sassoon; and raise money for charity by running the London Marathon.

There is nothing especially out of the ordinary about these goals and they don't have to be. Your goals simply need to be meaningful for you and motivate you to take action.

> Unfortunate are those without goals. For they drift along helping someone else to achieve theirs.

SUMO wisdom

The personal stuff

In 1996 I wrote down in some detail the house I wanted to live in. I knew the location I wanted, the type of garden, the number of bedrooms and the need for a kitchen big enough to eat in as a family. And I wanted a conservatory. The house we bought four years later did not have all we wanted but it was in the right location and had the right size garden. Two years later with the help of an extension we achieved our desired outcome. The future can be yours to see, but you need to plan for it.

Having decided what you want to do, the following questions will help you clarify how to make your goals a reality.

The third question is …

Have you shared your goals with someone close to you?

It is important you do not set goals in isolation. How supportive are those closest to you about your goals? When I was thinking of my ideal house, Helen, my wife, had some different ideas from me. Fortunately we agreed on most things, which was just as well, as we wanted to carry on living together. It has also been important that Helen supports my business goals, which to be achieved will mean my being away from home on a regular basis.

Likewise I need to be aware she has some goals that require my support. We may need to give and take a little on occasions and make some compromises. But it is far better for a long-term healthy relationship if we consider the needs of each other rather than single-mindedly pursuing our own objectives.

The fourth question is …

Do you have some plans in place to help you achieve your goals?

I regularly hear people say 'Well, we hope one day to …' or, 'Maybe one day we will have enough money to …' Can I be blunt about this?

Hope is not a strategy.

SUMO wisdom

Forget the phrase 'Show me the money' – I say, 'First show me the plan'. What's your strategy going to be to achieve your goals? Here are some questions to help you focus on what you want to achieve and how to go about making it a reality.

1   Why is this goal important to you? If you do not have a strong enough reason, your commitment to achieving your goal will be lessened. There is no point setting a half-hearted goal just for the sake of it.

2   What will it mean to you personally to achieve this goal? How will you feel when you reach your desired outcome?

3   Make an honest assessment of where you are currently in relation to your goal. Is it realistic to achieve your outcome and if so, in what time scale? (Setting yourself a target to earn a million pounds in the next six months when you are currently in debt, and there is no business opportunity on the horizon, is not impossible; but it's worth a reality check. And wanting to run a marathon in the next three months when you are currently struggling to climb the stairs is not advisable.) This is not a call to lower your aspirations, but be aware of the following:

SUMO wisdom

Start with the molehill, then build the mountain.

I think it is fantastic to dream big, but it is useful to start small. The first talk I ever gave was to a church youth group. Due to the evening running later than planned, my 'Thought For The Day' slot was reduced from five minutes to thirty seconds. Although I dreamed of speaking internationally, I started my speaking career in a church hall a mile away from home.

Start where you are
with what you have
and never lose sight of your dream.

SUMO
wisdom

Anthony Robbins offers a useful insight:

> *'People tend to overestimate what they can achieve in a year, but underestimate what they can achieve in a lifetime.'*

4 What resources do you need to help you achieve your goal? Resources could be in the form of equipment, money, time, information and people. People are perhaps your biggest resource. They can provide you with advice, introduce you to the appropriate contacts and support you in your journey. List your resources here:

The resources I need to help me achieve my goal:

5 Plan your plan. What needs to happen now? What is your next step and what about the one after that? What are your time scales?

The personal stuff

My goal this year was to write a book that incorporated the SUMO success principles that I had been speaking about through my work. This is the book you are now reading. In order to achieve this outcome I sought the help of my friend Steve. He suggested which publishers to approach and how best to pitch my proposal. I shared this goal with the people close to me, including my family, friends and colleagues from my industry. Having done so, I felt even more focused on making it a reality. I researched the publishers, started gathering my ideas and then began writing.

Along the journey I have had to deal with rejection as well as interest from publishers. I have listened to people challenge my ideas as well as support them. I have needed to write when I felt little or no inspiration and to see my task not as writing a book, but writing a page, followed by another page and then another. Not only have I been writing about the SUMO success principles, but I have been seeking to apply them as well. Rejection has brought the temptation to try on the Victim T-Shirt. I have resisted. Just. But I have appreciated the need to have a little Hippo Time with myself. I have heard the Inner Critic on numerous occasions but I have decided not to entertain him as a guest.

This has only been possible due to the support and encouragement of others. In fact without it, this book would never have been completed. I have remembered the beachball and sought the views of several people for their perspective on each chapter. They have seen 'sides' to each principle that I had not considered, they have given me insights into my own material that I had failed to notice.

I have also needed to remind myself on several occasions why writing this book is so important to me. There are several reasons, including a desire to see the SUMO message spread beyond the people who hear me speak. I confess I also want the book to raise my profile, which in my business is especially important. I also want to leave a legacy to my children, my grandchildren and their grandchildren. Though they may never meet me face to face, I hope they encounter me through the written pages. I guess the quote from my friend Nigel Risner, 'If you want to live an immortal life, do something worth remembering,' was particularly relevant and inspiring for me.

Points to ponder

This is a little of my story on the journey to achieve my goal. What will your story be? How will you use the SUMO principles to help you achieve success? What do you need to be aware of that could be an obstacle to your progress?

Finally, the fifth question ...

What kind of memories would you like your family and friends to have of you?

Write below what you believe they would say. If you are struggling, you might want to ask them. If you think there are not as many happy memories as you would like, then it is up to you to change that.

At the moment my family's memories of me would include:

In the future, I'd also like them to remember me because of:

At the moment my friends' memories of me would include:

In the future, I'd also like them to remember me because of:

In a nutshell

Designing your life and creating circumstances rather than reacting to them is not always easy. To do so means not simply reading about these SUMO principles, but living them as well.

It begins when we 'change our T-shirt' and acknowledge that if life is not as we want it, then creating a different future is down to us. It means taking charge of our thinking. Our thinking ultimately creates our results. When you want to make changes in life, 'faulty thinking' will anchor you to your old way of behaving. 'Fruity thinking' will release you to move forward. Use the seven questions in Chapter 2 to help your journey.

When setbacks occur, as they inevitably will, remember that 'Hippo Time is OK'. Don't deny your frustration or disappointment. Remember successful people do not go around succeeding all the time. Hippo Time can be helpful, but it can also hinder you. It is part of the journey – it is not a destination. Be careful who you spend it with and remember to *Move On*.

Appreciate that your journey is a much richer experience when you engage the support of others. Remind yourself that understanding their view of the beachball will enhance the quality of your relationships. Never forget that life is not simply about getting your needs met, but helping other people meet theirs. Never underestimate the incredible importance of listening and seeking to understand others.

Use the 'Learn Latin' principle to develop the motivation and momentum to move on. Remember, one of the biggest obstacles to overcoming any challenge is the first step. So just start. And make sure you have a mate to help you along the way.

Finally, 'Ditch Doris Day'. What your future looks like is largely down to you. Widen your definition of success and recognize that a more fulfilling future awaits you when you focus on your Career, Relationships, Recreation and Contribution.

And above all, in all things, remember to SUMO!

SUMO summary

- *Shut Up* the 'whatever will be, will be' attitude and *Move On* to creating your own future.
- Don't wait until it's too late to decide how to live the rest of your days.
- If you want more success in life, define what that means to you.
- *Shut Up* a narrow view of success and *Move On* to broaden your definition.
- Make sure you give your own life a regular service.
- Work–life fulfilment comes when we pay attention to our Career (or work), Relationships, Recreation and Contribution.
- Don't live your life by default. Set goals to create a sense of purpose and direction in your life.
- Create memories worth remembering.
- Dream big, start small.
- *Shut Up* believing success will just happen, *Move On* to develop a plan to create it.
- Use all six SUMO principles to create the future you want to see.

SUMO in Africa

Sometimes a door opens that you're not even pushing. Throughout 2005 my close friend Paul Sandham had been visiting Kenya, working in a voluntary capacity, providing leadership training and general support and encouragement to a host of Church and community leaders. During one such visit, he met a woman called Florence. She shared her passion for personal development and her desire to see more Kenyans motivated to make a difference in their communities. Paul in turn began to talk about his friend 'The Sumo Guy' and having brought several copies of the book *SUMO: Shut Up, Move On* out to Kenya, was happy to pass on a copy of the book to Florence. Twelve weeks after that chance conversation, I presented the first ever Sumo seminar in Kenya.

During my trip I spent the first few days of January visiting rural villages and spending time at a children's orphanage located on the outskirts of a town called Kisumu. The Kenyan summer gave me a chance to wear my SUMO T-shirt (I never miss an opportunity to promote the message!) and it wasn't long before I began to hear the greeting 'Jambo Sumo' (Hello Sumo).

The night before the seminar I met Florence for the first time. She had taken a big risk running such an event, but her contacts in the business community paid off. I had expected some sparsely furnished church hall to be the venue for my Sumo seminar, but Florence exceeded my expectations, slightly! In fact the Windsor Golf and Country Club, a five-star residence that had counted among its previous guests Nelson Mandela and Kofi Annan, proved to be the ideal venue and provided a taste of luxury I would struggle to find in Britain. Armed with a suitcase full of books (shipping them over was too expensive) I waited slightly nervously for proceedings to begin.

The first participants arrived just after 8am. Hopes were high that we would reach 50 delegates, but by 9am 70 people had registered and the hotel was busily sorting out extra tables and chairs. Three participants had travelled from Tanzania (a 15-hour journey by bus) in order to attend my friend Paul's Leadership Workshop (delivered the previous day) and The Sumo Seminar. There were even delegates from Rwanda and Ethiopia who were currently studying in Nairobi and who were intrigued by what the day entailed.

My main concern was how my six Sumo principles, written from a Western mindset and perspective, would relate to a different culture. Well,
key messages such as 'Change Your T-Shirt' (Take
responsibility for your life) and 'Develop Fruity
Thinking' (Take charge of your thinking) were
lapped up by my audience and I quickly realized
that my Sumo principles are principles for life no
matter what the culture or the context. At the
end of a long day, I left the venue with no books
(sold at a specially discounted rate, courtesy of
Capstone), some incredible memories and further invitations to spread the Sumo message in
Africa. Considering I could have been back in the
UK watching Bradford City lose to Chesterfield, I
sensed this visit to Kenya had been a rather good
decision.

Paul McGee spreads the SUMO message in Africa

The Personal Postscript

Let me end by sharing a few final thoughts that I hope reinforce some of the messages around SUMO.

Several years ago, an incident occurred one night that will live with me until the day I die. Helen had been rushed into hospital with appendicitis. The doctors wanted to operate immediately. Whilst Helen was being prepared for theatre, the nurse took a note of our personal details and informed me that as the next of kin, I would be the first to be contacted in an emergency. We were living in a rented flat at the time and were not on the telephone (and this was before people had mobiles), so I was reassuringly informed that if there was a life or death situation and the hospital needed to contact me urgently, they would send a policeman round to the flat.

I left the hospital after Helen returned from theatre and although she was groggy – she even refused chocolate – the operation appeared to have been a success. I returned home, caught up with the news and went to bed. It was nearly midnight. At three o'clock in the morning, my doorbell rang. It took me a moment to realize Helen was not with me and then as the doorbell rang a second time, I remembered the words of the nurse, '… only in a life or death situation'.

I felt a strange mix of both calm and overwhelming anxiety as I walked out of our flat on the first floor and across the landing to the main stairway. As I went down the stairs to open the main door, I remember thinking, 'Be a tramp, be a drunk, just don't be a policeman'. I realized that if it was a policeman calling at that time of night, it could only be for one reason. I opened the door and there stood a policeman.

'I'm looking for a Mr McGee,' he explained.

'You've found him.'

'Sir, I've got some bad news, do you mind if I come in?'

I don't remember replying. As the realization of what he said sank in, I simply turned to go back up the stairs. After just one year of marriage Helen was gone. I was in shock. As we entered the flat I sat down and finally spoke.

'It's about Helen, isn't it?'

The policeman looked at me rather confused and said, 'Who?'

'Helen, my wife … they said at the hospital that …'

'Sir', he interrupted, 'I don't know anything about your wife, but do you own a Peugeot 104?'

Now I was the one who was confused. 'Yes, why?'

'Well, Mr McGee, it's been stolen and left abandoned about ten miles from here. They've smashed in the windscreen and made a right mess of it internally.'

'Really?' I replied in tones of semi-ecstasy.

'Did you know your car had been stolen, sir? It's just that your reaction is rather unusual.'

I felt like dancing! I wanted to hug this bearer of such great news. Helen was alive – it was just a stupid car that had been stolen.

That incident served to remind me of what is of real lasting value in my life. Possessions can be replaced, people can't. It provided perspective. The SUMO question, 'How important is this issue on a scale of 1–10?' has never been so pertinent since that night. It reminds me that creating and enjoying a brilliant life is something I want to experience with someone close to me, and yet how easy it is for the less important stuff to dominate my attention. I hope that I have conveyed that one of the underlying messages of SUMO is *focus on what is important.* That is much harder to do when you haven't stopped to think about what actually is important to you. Make sure you do.

A few months after that incident I lost my job through ill health. I had no job, no income and no prognosis of when, or if, I would make a full recovery. It forced me to stop and think. I had no idea if I would ever recover my health again, and the only person I knew with my condition (ME, or chronic fatigue syndrome) was confined to a wheelchair. I determined then, that whether I recovered or not, I would make the most of my life. I believe it is a conscious decision we all need to make.

Two and a half years later I started my own business. It was not a difficult decision to make. I still wasn't well enough to pass a medical, so the only way I could work was to hire myself. Yet it amazes me how quickly I forgot the challenges of my past and how soon I began to take my life and my health for granted again. Gradually though, I am waking up to the fact that life is a privilege and along with that privilege comes opportunity and responsibility. Alvin Law, a Canadian motivational speaker, was born with no arms as a result of his mother taking the drug thalidomide during pregnancy. I felt profoundly challenged by him when he said, 'The mirror does not accurately reflect who we are; our lives do.' I believe if we don't *S*hut *U*p and *M*ove *O*n from certain things, then we are robbing ourselves and others of living a fulfilling and meaningful life.

As for my hopes for the future, my passionate desire is that the SUMO philosophy does not just become a memorable catch phrase, but that it provokes us to *M*ove *O*n to making a difference in our lives and the lives of others. In the words of Paul Scanlon, who leads an inner city church in Bradford: 'I want to live full, die empty.' I want to create and enjoy a brilliant life, but wouldn't it be great if we could help others do the same?

Let me leave you with this thought. You may remember watching quiz shows when the contestant fails to win the main prize. At the end of the programme, the still-smiling quiz master proclaims, 'Look what you could have won', as the major prize (often a boat or a motor car) is revealed. The contestant forces a smile, but the disappointment can be seen in their eyes. At the end of my show on this planet, I don't want to be told, 'Look what you could have won. Look what you could have done. Look what you could have become.'

I hope SUMO helps you to create and enjoy an even better life than you have now. I hope it helps you achieve better relationships with others and inspires you to attempt things you only ever dreamed of doing. I hope above all it leaves you looking back on your life and saying, 'Look what I've won, look what I've done, look who I've become.' It's not an easy journey, as I have already found, but it's a journey worth taking.

Let me know how SUMO helps.

Carpe diem.

Paul McGee

Want to know more about SUMO?

If you want to know more about SUMO, then visit www.TheSumoGuy.com. You can nominate people for SUMO awards, share your thoughts on how SUMO has helped you and learn how it has helped others.

Find out which charities have benefited from the proceeds of this book and discover how you can get hold of other SUMO products.

You can also pose a question online to Paul and find out when and where Paul is speaking in your area.

SUMO in schools

Finally, Paul is keen to hear from anyone who is interested in developing and using the SUMO principles inside schools. If that's you, then be sure to make contact.

Visit www.TheSumoGuy.com
or e-mail sumo@paulmcgee.com

Bring Paul to your organization

Paul McGee speaks at team events, conferences and – if you really twist his arm – at after-dinner functions. The topics he speaks on include Motivation, Leadership, Customer Service and Succeeding Through Change.

You can book Paul or one of his team to deliver the principles of this book inside your organization. For more details about the SUMO programme or any more of Paul's services, either:

e-mail: sumo@paulmcgee.com

or visit: www.paulmcgee.com
or www.TheSumoGuy.com

If you prefer, you can telephone the offices of PMA International Ltd (Paul's company) on

tel: +44 (0) 1925 268708

We look forward to hearing from you.

SUMO and UNICEF

Some people who want to 'Move On' in life are hindered through no fault of their own. Therefore I have decided that part of the profits from this book will go to UNICEF.

UNICEF, the United Nations Children's Fund, is the world's largest organization working specifically for children, protecting and promoting their rights. It works in 157 countries of the world to help every child reach their full potential through long term and emergency work on child health and nutrition, quality basic education for all boys and girls, and the protection of children from violence, exploitation and HIV/AIDS.

By working in partnership with others, from governments and teachers to youth groups and mothers, UNICEF is a driving force for people throughout the world working to ensure a better world for children.

UNICEF receives no funding from the UN and relies entirely on voluntary donations to fund its work. UNICEF needs financial support to help protect children from exploitation and to build a world fit for children. You can make a difference.

If you are in the UK and would like to find out about how you can support UNICEF, please visit www.unicef.org.uk.

Everyone deserves the opportunity for a better tomorrow. By purchasing this book you are playing your part in making that happen for thousands of children around the world. Thank you.

Paul McGee

Index